CONTENTS

Reader's Needs

THINK LIKE GOOGLE

How to use SEO & empathy to rank, convert, and profit no matter how much they change the rules

by Tom Gerencer

Copyright 2019 by Gerencer Creative, Inc.

For Kathy, Maddox, and Ben

INTRODUCTION

What's the single most important thing about SEO?

Is it keywords? Backlinks? Time on page?

In short, *what does Google want?*

In the 2000 romantic comedy *What Women Want,* Mel Gibson plays a sexist executive who gains the magical ability to hear women's thoughts. He uses it to understand Helen Hunt. Hijinx, hilarity, and romance ensue.

The movie was a kind of dramatization of the then-popular *Mars and Venus* books, in which relationship counselor John Gray explains that if we only understood each other better, we'd get along.

I first read those books on the advice of a friend. I didn't want to but his description was compelling.

"It's like someone gave me a pair of glasses from that movie *They Live,*" he said, "and suddenly everything was clear to me."

He was referring to the science fiction movie from director John Carpenter. In the film, wrestler "Rowdy" Roddy Piper plays a drifter who gets a special pair of sunglasses. With them, he can see that things are vastly different than they seem.

This book will give you a pair of *They Live* glasses to see into Google's mind. Read it, and all your nagging questions about SEO will vanish. Practice it, and your pages will rank high in Google no matter how often they change the rules.

SEO's Sea Change

The hard fact is, journalists *need* to be SEO experts. In February of 2019, 2,300 journalists lost their jobs at BuzzFeed, Yahoo!, Gannett, Vice, and other online outlets. Why?

Because of what Google is doing. Because SEO is *changing how we consume and produce content, radically.*

In the days of words on paper, when the dinosaurs of old journalism roamed free, brandishing four-color teeth, journalism was a simple process. Publishers hired editors — smart people with a knack for seeing into readers' hearts. They were savants at empathy. They could listen to a pitch, chew their big, disgusting cigars, and say in microseconds, "Nobody cares," or, "It's sensational!" and be right 99.99999% of the time.

The publishers produced such gripping, talked-about publications that everybody wanted a copy on the coffee table. It became a game of eyeballs. Advertisers flocked in. They said, "Tell your readers about our products and we'll pay you piles of money!"

The editors could take that money and hire the best writers, photographers, and illustrators. Everyone was happy.

Except nothing lasts forever.

The internet came along. Bloggers popped up like digital prairie dogs across the yellowed landscape. They chimed in with alternate and often unwelcome viewpoints. They called out mistakes or outright lies from the established media. And the eyeballs started turning toward them. You could almost see the old-world publishers and editors, sitting in their ivory towers, mouths hung open around disgusting cigars, saying, "What's going on?"

As the eyeballs turned, the ads and money followed. Thus began the slow, relentless march away from print.

Now online editors sit in their digital ivory towers. They can hear a pitch, chew their disgusting biscotti, and say instinctively, "It's viral!" or "Nobody cares!" Except in the past few years companies are asking, "Hey, what are we doing? Why are we paying BuzzFeed and HuffPost for ad space? Why can't we just DIY our content for a fraction of the cost?" So they're doing that, undermining the massive edifice of traditional web journalism so it crumbles like a calving glacier.

But wait a second. How can this work? What about the genius editors? The savants who know what people want to read? Are there enough of them to go around? How can every company hire one, from the massive multinational down to the tiny startup? Sure, when *Time* and *Newsweek* were our leading source of content, there were sufficient editors with their fingers on the pulse to fill the need.

But what about now, when every little mom-and-pop is doing their own content? Are there enough genius empaths who know intuitively what people want to read? Enough to compete on a national level? There can't be, right?

Well, here's the dark and secret heart of SEO:

There don't have to be.

Ready for a shock? Google is your new editor. This is why SEO is so vital to content creators today. We *need to master* SEO because *it's the only way to please Google.* And Google is pushing all those brilliant editors out of their ivory towers. It's sitting in their chairs and chewing its disgusting data packets and seeing straight into the heart of every reader. It can look at an article or post and say, "Nobody cares," or, "It's #1!"

That can't be true.

Can it?

How could a machine possibly have more empathy than most human beings?

To paraphrase James Cromwell from the 2004 Will Smith film *I, Robot,* now you're asking the right question. Understand the answer and you'll understand SEO.

PART 1: TO RANK IN GOOGLE, THINK LIKE GOOGLE

CHAPTER 1: SEO IS LIKE EATING ROCKS

Why is SEO so hard?

It's maddening.

You need to rank.

You don't *just* need to rank. You need to rank page 1.

You don't *just* need to rank page 1. You need to rank at the *top of page 1.*

And while we're at it, could you have a featured snippet?

In the Google results, only 8% of searchers even *look at* page 2. That means 92% of all search traffic goes to the top 10 articles in Google Search.

If you're already the top result in the SERPs (Search Engine Result Pages) congratulations! You get 33% of all the traffic. According to a study from marketing site Chitika.com, that drops to 17% for article #2, 11% for #3, and so on. By the time we hit the 10th article, only 2.4% of searchers even look at it. The remaining 8% get spread over all the other millions of results, all crying out in the wilderness.

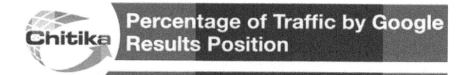

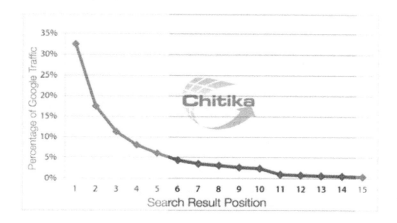

But it's *so hard* to rank on that first page, let alone get the top result or featured snippet—especially for the little guy.

The big contenders suck the oxygen out of the internet's living room. The *Business Insiders* and the *WebMDs*, the *CNNs* and *Forbes* and *HuffPosts* take the lion's share of traffic, elbowing out everybody else. They've got the low Alexa ranks and the high site authorities, and if they dominate your topics, good luck squirming in. You're like a runt pig, shoving and wriggling for the right to stay alive, while brawnier contenders do their level best to starve you out.

So, you read books and articles about SEO. You learn to use keywords. But not too many keywords because Google doesn't like that. You learn to get backlinks. But not too many backlinks because Google doesn't like that.

Then finally you figure out the right SEO formula to rank. It's working! Your monthly views are going up!

Until Google rolls out the next Panda, Penguin, Pigeon, or other alliteratively-named update and your traffic crashes down into the pits of hell again.

It Happened to Me

Several years ago, I was hired by a web publishing firm to be the head (and only) writer for a brand new money site. They gave me just enough rope to hang myself. "Here," they said, "write five articles a week—2,250 words each, and we'll pay you $40,000 a year."

My wife Kathy and I had just moved to the middle of nowhere and she was ten months pregnant with our first son. That $40,000 seemed like manna from heaven.

The only rules were: 1) I had to be ethical 2) I had to create my own topics, and 3) I had to get traffic.

I worked hard. In the first three months I got a whopping 360 readers. But gradually, I learned the ropes. In six months I was outranking articles by *Forbes* and *Fortune*. A combination of good keyword placement and solid original content got me noticed. By 17 months I'd built a solid base of 600,000 readers a month. In month 18 that spiked to 800,000, I was overjoyed.

Then things plateaued. We dropped back to 600,000 and hung there for two months. And then disaster struck.

What happened? I still don't know. I contend that switching the website to the Google AMP (a technical move that doesn't matter here) hurt us fatally. My boss was adamant the Trump election made Google lash out at thousands of websites in a kind of digital McCarthyism. In other words, Google blacklisted us (albeit unjustly) as "fake news."

Whatever the reason, we lost 90% of our traffic overnight. We went from page 1 for most of our articles to page 2 or 3. Six weeks later we were still tanking when I got the bad news. My boss called and told me he was shuttering the project. Myself, my editor, and another writer who'd just been hired all lost our jobs. I was the sole breadwinner in our family. It was three weeks after Christmas and Kathy had just had another baby.

To say I was depressed is understatement. What right did Google have to blacklist us, apparently at random?

Well, every right. Because they're the only game in town. They're the company that made search possible. So yeah, they own it.

So What Can We Do?

A long time before the money website crashed, I made my first foray into eCommerce. I wanted to sell my funny safety videos online. I didn't know anything about how to get people to find me. I didn't even know what SEO meant.

I did what I always do in those situations. I asked a friend for help. In this case it was my pal Kevin Ladd, CEO of the popular site Scholarships.com.

"Does Google have like a manual for how to get your page to show up?" I said, naively.

"No," Kevin said.

"Well, why not?"

"Because Google doesn't want you gaming them."

That statement has echoed around in my head for years.

Google doesn't want us figuring out its tricks. It doesn't even *like* search engine optimization, because to some extent that's *tricking* Google.

Ralph Waldo Emerson once said there are a million methods,

but few principles. "The man who grasps principles," he said, "can successfully select his own methods." Meanwhile, those who try methods without principles will fail.

Focusing on the tactics and techniques of SEO is a dead end to zero traffic. Focusing on what Google wants is the swift road to success.

So, what *does* Google want?

It wants you to think like it does.

Well, what if that's our goal? What if, instead of struggling to keep on top of Google updates, we ignore the updates and we try to hit the same goal Google's aiming for? What if we focus on the reason behind all those annoying changes to its algorithm?

The question makes me think of that scene in *Raising Arizona* where the parole board grills H.I. McDonough.

"You're not just telling us what we want to hear, are you boy?"

"No sir, I wouldn't do that" McDonough says.

"Cause we just want to hear the truth."

"Well, then I guess I *am* telling you what you want to hear."

"Boy, didn't we just tell you not to do that?"

"Yessir."

"Okay then."

Google in this case is your parole board. You're H.I. McDonough, right down to your shock of *Something About Mary* hair. Ranking high in Google and making piles of profit is your parole from the penitentiary of no-traffic.

What Google Wants

So if Google doesn't want us "doing SEO," what *does* it want?

It wants us to forget the keywords and the SEO and serve the reader. It wants us to deliver what the *reader* wants. It can't enforce that yet. It's not smart enough. But it's getting closer with each update.

I got my first clue many years ago from Steve Krug's excellent web design book, Don't Make Me Think.

If you haven't read it, it's worth the money. I stumbled on it while building my first eCommerce website.

I was proud of that site. I learned PHP and MySQL to create it, along with Javascript, HTML, CSS, and other odds and ends.

Better still, the site followed Krug's advice: people are busy and have lots of options, so when you design your website, don't make them think. If you do, you'll lose them.

That idea gets at something buried in the secret heart of SEO. Namely, a desire to *serve the reader.*

Between Krug's advice not to make the user think, and Peter Kent's advice on keywords in *SEO for Dummies*, I got my site to rank at #1 in Google. But along the way I made some good choices that weren't in either book. Those choices came down to *how* I used my keywords and design.

Keywords Are a Giant Pain

The very thought of keywords ought to make you shudder.

There's something nasty about letting a machine generate a spreadsheet crammed with terms to work into our writing. The whole idea is antiseptic. It ain't natural. It undercuts the reason we write in the first place.

So—why do we write? Why do you? Why did you set out to create great content or great journalism, aside from needing to pay rent? If you're like most, it's because you want to tell stories and share information you think people need to know. You want, in other words, to *serve the reader.*

Where do keywords enter into that?

They don't. At least, not the way most people think.

In fact, in the past few years, Google has been focusing less and less on keywords. It would *love* to ditch them altogether. In fact it *is* ditching them, more and more with every update. I'll get into how it's doing that soon. For now, you should know that if you focus on keywords, you may succeed for a while, but it'll erode out from under you like beach sand dumped on coastline by the Army Corps of Engineers.

So, if keywords aren't the end-all, be-all, then what *should* we focus on?

10x Content is a Pain

In 2015, the best advice for how to rank was to create "10x content." SEO guru Rand Fishkin coined the phrase in one of his popular *Whiteboard Friday* presentations.

What's 10x content?

It's content 10 times better than anything else out there. It's necessary, Fishkin says, because there's so much competition. And a lot of it is frighteningly good.

15 years ago, all we had to do was put some garbage on the internet with the right keywords and we'd rank. Are you writing about flapper valves? Well, put the terms "flapper valve" and "valves that flap" throughout your article, lots of times. This produced some awkward reading, but when you're the only game in town, your game doesn't have to be that great.

Thankfully we can't do that anymore. There's more and more good content. The garbage falls through the cracks.

With 10x content, the idea is, if you write something *10 times better* than what everybody else is writing, you'll stand out. Even better, you'll have staying power. It'll take a long time before the other pretenders knock you off your digital throne. It's kind of like breaking an Olympic track record by a few fractions of a second vs breaking it by a minute-and-a-half.

There's a clue here. How does Google know the difference between 10x content and 1x content? Is it because 10x content has 10 times more keywords? Or is something else at work? Whatever it is, 10x content certainly did seem to work.

But there's a problem. What happens when *everyone* is writing 10x content? What happens in a couple years, when *all* the content is 10x? How long can we keep one-upping ourselves? Is that sustainable? And do web users really want that?

A couple years ago I Googled "outboard motor won't start." I was at the boat launch on a busy Sunday with my dog barking and the baby crying and the 2-year-old throwing crudite and pieces of the boat into the lake. Kathy looked like she was wondering how long it would take me to bleed out if she hit me with the hibachi. Did I really want to read a piece of 10x content at that point? Did I really need the most comprehensive piece of literature about flooded engines on the web?

Or did I just want someone to say, "Here's why your outboard motor isn't starting and how to fix it fast?"

Plus, 10x content is expensive. It's exhausting. If you're the writer, doing ever-more research and writing ever-better content is a lovely goal, but unsustainable. If you have to spend more time on each successive piece, how can you make a living? Or if you're *hiring* writers, will you have to constantly 10x their pay?

So What the Heck?

So where does all this leave us?

If keywords aren't the holy grail, and writing better and longer content is unsustainable, what can we do? How can we supply what Google wants? In a nutshell, how can we excel at SEO?

That's what this book is all about. Let's get at the answer, next.

CHAPTER 2: WHAT GOOGLE WANTS

Many years ago I wrote a short science fiction story about a robot that develops empathy.

It got my first long, thoughtful rejection from Gordon Van Gelder, then editor at the *Magazine of Fantasy and Science Fiction*. That was huge to me, because I'd been trying to break into that market for years. So far the best I'd managed was a terse "This didn't work for me, alas."

This time I got a two page letter saying why the story almost worked. Van Gelder liked the idea of a robot with more empathy than any human (with the possible exception of Jesus and the Buddha). It was a radical idea back then, but is it really all that radical today? Machines improve dramatically with every generation. It's not science fiction to say they're learning to outperform us in every way. They're already faster than us (cars, airplanes, rockets) and stronger than us (backhoes, dump trucks, hydraulic presses). Most tech gurus believe one day they'll be smarter than us too.

So—why wouldn't they outdo us at emotion?

Am I saying Google has done that? Well, no. If you've read anything about the current state of AI, you know we're a long way from where machines can out-empathize us. Just take a look at LinkedIn's auto-responses and you'll see what I mean. (Last week someone asked me if I could help them immigrate to Canada and LinkedIn suggested I say, "Sure!" "lol" or "I'm not sure.")

But it turns out Google doesn't have to *understand* empathy to deliver it.

Here's how it works. Once you get it, your understanding of SEO will change dramatically.

Google's Goal

Google's goal is making money. There, I said it.

They want to make Scrooge McDuck-sized piles of money and go swimming in it.

Or they want to use it to R&D ways to help the human race in a completely altruistic fashion.

Take your pick.

Either way, this is capitalism. Regardless of their stated mission, they're a publicly traded corporation whose job is to make money for their shareholders. (Without being evil, of course.)

Notwithstanding the fees they collect from Google Drive upgrades and the take from Chromecast and other side efforts, their biggest moneymaker by far is ad revenue.

So—how can Google earn the most ad cash?

By delivering what searchers want. A searcher says, "Who's that guy in Hogan's Heroes with the test tubes bubbling in the opening credits?" Google tells them and earns ad revenue.

So how does Google give those searchers what they want?

It doesn't tell us. But we have some pretty compelling clues.

At first it had to use keywords. If you typed in "best breakfast cereals" Google knew it had to show articles that contained the words "best" and "breakfast cereals" a lot.

But people started cheating. People started stuffing in those words like crazy to outperform the other pages. There was no real measure of which page served the searcher's needs the best.

There was only a measure of which page had the right keywords the most times.

So Google started refining things. If you put too many key-words in an article, they'd penalize you by shunting your page down to the second or third page of the search results.

But that wasn't perfect either. Google still didn't do a good enough job putting the "best" page up top. That is, the page that served the searcher in the best way. So they kept working on it.

Big Google is Watching You

Does Google scare you?

Google has access to an insane amount of data on our search habits. I'm writing this at 7am. I just checked InternetLiveStats.com, and they say Google has had 1.98 billion searches so far today. (I did about 30 of them myself.) The same site estimates 73,259 searches every second.

Google doesn't just let those searches flit by without noticing. It pays attention. It watches how people use it. How do I know?

Well, Google doesn't let us look in through a peephole at its inner workings. Nobody at Google says, "Hey everybody, here's how we use user data to get better."

Still, there are some pretty solid theories about how Google works. One I happen to agree with is *dwell time.*

Google Is a Voting Booth

Without putting on a white lab coat and a pair of Buddy Holly glasses, dwell time is just how long someone spends on a page. I could get into terms like time-on-page, bounce rate, or session duration, but I won't. (Thank me with cash.) Basically the the-ory goes like this:

Let's say I'm searching Google. I'm interested in what causes tantrums. My two-year old has been screaming a lot lately and

I'd like to know why.

So, I Google it:

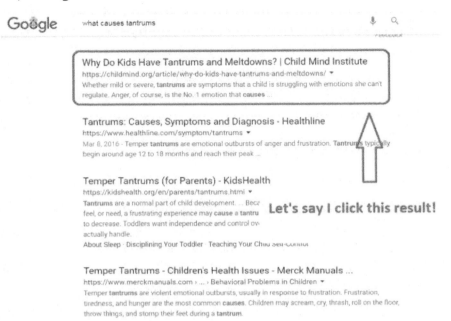

(Source: Google.com)

I get some good results. The top one looks as good as any, so I click it. Turns out that top article is excellent. It answers all my questions. It gives me solid tips to help my Benny boy. It tells me all kinds of things I didn't *know* I needed to know. It's engaging, well-written, and chock full of everything I need.

In fact, the article is so good I stay there for 15 minutes, thoroughly engrossed and learning, watching videos, and looking at informative and helpful diagrams. Then I click the "back" button and look at another article.

Well, Google sees that. It sees me search for "what causes tantrums" and it sees me click that top result. It sees me come back 15 minutes later and click something else.

Now Google thinks, "Well, that must be a pretty good page, as far as Tom is concerned. He stayed there a long time."

Or maybe I don't like the article. I click through to it, decide it doesn't help, and click "back" three seconds later. Google sees that, too. Or maybe I click into it and *never* go back to Google. The point is, Google watches me and gathers information in the background about which articles I probably like and which I don't. It makes assumptions based on my behavior.

Based on those assumptions, it floats the pages I like a little higher in the search results, and the ones I don't a little lower.

Now picture Google going through that process not just with me for that one search, but with six billion searches every day.

Seen that way, Google is less like an algorithm for analyzing keyword placement and more like a giant voting booth. Every time you click an article and read it, you're voting for it and against the others.

There's some debate in the SEO community about whether Google really works this way. Some say it would be too easy to manipulate. Others point out Google's blind spots. It doesn't know, for instance, how much time you actually spend reading a page. Maybe you got up and made a sandwich. It doesn't know if the page really helped you. Maybe it just frustrated you for 15 minutes.

That aside, I strongly believe this is how Google thinks. Part of that comes from writing over 1,500 published web articles and watching how they ranked. I changed my approach slightly with each attempt and tracked my progress through the years. One constant has held true for all those articles: The better I understood the reader and the harder I worked to serve her, the higher my articles have ranked.

When I first started writing for the web, I'd pack my articles with keywords. I'm ashamed to say I had to write a lot of net worth articles for a couple years. To get them to rank, I'd put "Justin Bieber net worth" or "Hillary Clinton net worth" in the first sentence. Then I'd put it in the headings. Then I'd put it 10 times in a bulleted list somewhere in the introduction.

Putting the keywords in *a lot,* I reasoned, was the best way to rank high. And it worked.

But I started to notice something. My articles would invariably rank high in Google right away. I'd make it into the top slot, or the #2 or #3 spot, within a few days—most of the time.

But then something weird would happen. Some of my articles would drift higher, while others gradually sank. I wrote hundreds of net worth articles. They all had the same pattern of keywords. But I started to see a common theme.

Almost always, when an article floated higher, it had better writing, better information, and it was more engaging.

Almost always, when an article sank lower, I'd gone through the motions, phoning in my work.

What was happening? The keyword placement was the same. How could Google know a weak article from a strong one?

Well, because the readers knew. I started to suspect that Google was originally placing all my posts high in the ranking because of good keyword placement. But then it was keeping them there (or letting them drop) based on whether *readers* liked them.

Here's a little more proof. In 2011, Duane Forrester, Senior Project Manager for Bing, said this about dwell time:

"Your goal should be that when a visitor lands on your page, the content answers all of their needs, encouraging their next action to remain with you. If your content does not encourage them to remain with you, they will leave. The search engines can get a sense of this by watching the dwell time. The time between when a user clicks on our search result and when they come back from your website tells a potential story. A minute or two is good as it can easily indicate the visitor consumed your content. Less than a couple of seconds can be viewed as a poor result. And while that's not the only factor we review when helping to determine quality, it's a signal we watch."

Now, Google gets about 65% of the internet's search traffic, while Bing (which powers Yahoo! search) gets 33%. So, Bing isn't Google. But if Bing is using this (smart) trick to rank pages, why wouldn't Google do it too?

Then there's this: In 2017, Nick Frost, the Head of Google Brain in Canada, said this about dwell time:

"So when search was invented, like when Google was invented many years ago, they wrote heuristics that figure out what the relationship between a search and the best page for that search was. And those heuristics worked pretty well and continue to work pretty well. But Google is now integrating machine learning into that process. So they're training models on when someone clicks on a page and stays on that page, or when they go back, or when—and trying to figure out exactly what that relationship is. So search is getting better and better and better because of advances in machine learning."

Now, Frost isn't the head of Google Search. He's the Head of Google Brain in Canada. But he most probably has some insight into what's going on with search in the rest of the company.

Google is almost certainly using the "wisdom of crowds" to judge the strength of web pages. That's the concept that large groups of people are often smarter than individuals or experts. Popularized by the James Surowiecki book, *The Wisdom of Crowds*, crowd wisdom is why single stock pickers are hard pressed to outperform the stock market.

Want to know more about dwell time? Check out Joshua Hardwick's excellent article in the ahrefs.com blog.

Forget the Rules

Regardless of whether Google uses dwell time or something

else, you'd better believe it's not blind to the oceans of user data passing through its servers every day. They've got access to a staggering amount of information about our search behavior and they can use it any way they want to pick the pages we like best.

Whether you believe in dwell time or not, you'd be hard put to reject my central premise: that A) Google wants to serve the reader, B) It's getting better and better at doing that, and C) Keywords were just the first attempt at getting that result.

So—even if you reject dwell time, understand it's just the tip of the iceberg. Google is probably working on other ways to use their mountains of user data to answer the question, "Which page best serves the reader?"

It's not always going to be dwell time. Try this for example. Google, "Is it Christmas?" The top result is a page called isitchristmas.com. Click through to it on any day but Christmas, and you'll see this:

NO

Now I ask you. How much time will you spend on that page? Not much, right? It gets a laugh. So clearly dwell time isn't why the page is #1. (In fact, it may be that it cracks people up, so it gets a lot of inbound links, but let's save that for a later chapter.)

The point is, Google is working hard every day to improve how they pick the pages we like best. Their goal is to serve the searcher as much as possible. They keep coming up with more efficient ways to do it. They keep rolling out updates to get closer to the goal. Those updates confound the content creators who are doing their damnedest to figure out the rules and game the system.

So, forget the rules. Forget the keywords and the dwell time and the gaming and the SEO. Forget all that and focus on what Google is focusing on. Think like Google. Serve the searcher.

CHAPTER 3: WHAT THE READER WANTS

So if Google wants what the searcher wants, and they're delivering it by watching two trillion searches per year, we have to ask, "What does the searcher want?"

How can we know?

Well I guess we just sit by our computers waiting until somebody searches for something. Then we call him on the phone and ask, "Hey, what exactly is it that you're looking for and why?"

Then the searcher will say, "I'm looking to find out how much money NFL referees make because I'm trying to win an argument with my annoying brother-in-law. He says they're way underpaid but I think that's garbage."

"Well," you'll say, "just sit tight while I go do some research and sort out the BS from the truth and figure out the best answer and I'll call you back OK? Might take me a couple hours."

Well OK, maybe if you had an infinite amount of time and so did the reader. But you don't and they don't. So in that case what do we do?

Sell Me This Keyboard

To answer that, I've got a little scenario for you. I promise it won't hurt.

Imagine you're in a conference room with 250 of your closest friends.

The consultant/speaker struts back and forth up front. He's clad in a $7,000 Kiton and a confident half-smile. His eyes gleam like garnets as he scans the room.

Suddenly he zeroes in on you.

A hush falls as he stalks forward and bends down. You can smell his cologne—something high-priced made from pressed *Kokia Cookei* and sperm whale remains.

Then he extends a Bic Cristal Up Ball pen.

"Sell me this pen," he says.

What do you do?

Well, you want to get up and walk out. In the first place, it's an annoying question. A sales-interviewer trick stolen from *The Wolf of Wall Street*. In the second, who wants to be put on the spot in a room crammed with people, all wondering if you'll fail?

But you've paid $1,100 for this seminar. So dutifully, you clear your throat and prepare to fail so you can help the speaker make his point.

What does this have to do with SEO?

To answer that, we'll have to get at the correct answer to the question.

So—what's the right answer to *Sell me this pen?*

I had to write that up recently in an article for career site *Zety.com*. My usual habit when I research an article is to dig into all the other articles out there and see what everybody else is saying. The top articles in the Google search results were flashy. Well-written. They had cool answers. But they weren't satisfying.

They all pointed to *The Wolf of Wall Street*. In fact, my keyword research had the movie's title right up there at the top.

All the articles said the question comes from the movie, and the best answer is right there in the script. They also gave the reason for the question.

The question, they said, is a sales interview technique. It works like this:

A hopeful sales job applicant sits down in the hotseat. The interviewer smiles. They exchange pleasantries. Then the interviewer leans forward and extends a pen.

"Sell me this pen," the interviewer says.

Then, depending on the answer, the interviewer knows that either A) the candidate has sales skills or B) she doesn't and deserves the old heave-ho.

The top articles in Google had it half right.

They were right that the question is a sales interview tool.

They were dead wrong that the best answer comes from *The Wolf of Wall Street*.

Umm... He's still not talking about SEO.

It's coming. And when it hits, you'll be able to think like Google. Not by the end of the book, but by the end of the chapter.

In the movie, the *sell me this pen* question pops up twice.

The first time is in the first few minutes. The antihero, Jordan Belfort, played by Leonardo DiCaprio, has designs on greatness. In a cafeteria with his other salesmen friends, he pops the question. After a little grousing, one of them obliges. He takes the pen, looks at it, and says, "Do me a favor. Write your name on that napkin."

"I don't have a pen," DiCaprio protests.

"Sold," the friend says. Everybody laughs.

Clever. But not the right answer.

The question shows up again at the end. Belfort has gone from riches to rags to jail and out again. He's now a sales consultant, stalking a conference room full of eager would-be sales reps.

Sound familiar?

"Sell me this pen," he asks one of them.

"Uh, it's a nice pen," the attendee gulps. "It's made of silver..."

Also the wrong answer. Talking about benefits isn't selling. Even I know that, and I'm not a sales rep.

My problem as the writer was this: I couldn't write my article the same as all the other articles. It wouldn't rank. But worse, it wouldn't offer any good advice. It would just parrot what the others said, which to my eyes wouldn't help my readers ace a sales interview. I had to give them something meaty they could sink their teeth into.

Then one article lower down the stack said the *real* answer was in Jordan Belfort's book, *Way of the Wolf*.

So, I bought the book on Kindle and did a quick search for the word "pen." There were 179 instances in the book. Flipping through them quickly, I found the right one. It was in a chapter where Belfort tells the story of a sales interview he gave during the height of his career as a master salesman and criminal.

An eager young applicant walked into Belfort's Wall Street office and sat down. Belfort sized the young man up, then handed him a pen and sprung the question.

"This is the most amazing pen money can buy!" the kid chirped. "It can write upside down! It'll never run out of ink! It feels great in your hand!"

He went on extolling the pen's benefits, finishing with "Whaddaya say?"

"You mean," said Belfort, "besides the fact that you're obviously completely full of shit?"

Belfort gave the kid a solid tongue-lashing, finishing with a clue to the real answer to the question:

"Did it ever occur to you," he said, "to maybe ask me a few questions before you attempted to ram a pen down my throat? Like, am I even in the market for a pen? Do I have a certain price range in mind? Do I prefer one type of pen to another?"

Pay attention. Get your arm hairs to stand up, because this is SEO. This is the key to thinking like Google.

Why?

Because it gets at the central question in all search content creation, which is the same as the central question in all sales.

Let's take a running start at it.

The sales interview question, "sell me this pen" isn't some kind of gimmick to see if you're a sales savant. It's not supposed to show your raw talent for shoveling BS. It's not supposed to prove you can hypnotize the Sahara into buying seven metric tons of sand.

What it's supposed to do is see if you have basic empathy.

That is: will you sell like a robot, extolling the product's benefits and making things up regardless of the reader's needs?

Or: will you try to get to know the other person's needs?

A good sales rep knows she has to have a *qualifying conversation* with each potential customer. That's where she steps up and asks, "Hey, do you need a pen? Do you like pens? Do you ever buy pens? What do you look for in a pen? What problems irk you about buying pens?"

In short, am I selling to the right person? If so, what does he really need?

If the sales rep knows her customer's needs, she can meet

them. She can work to help the person. Not try to ram some unwanted object down an unwilling throat.

Again, what does this have to do with SEO?

Everything.

Because this is exactly what Google is doing to everyone who publishes an article online. It's asking us, "Do you know enough about your reader? As a content creator, do you know why your reader sat down and typed those few words in the search box? In short, did it ever occur to you to ask the reader a few questions before you tried to ram an article down her throat?

Empathy Is the Key

This all boils down to empathy. To being able to understand at a gut level what the reader wants. The good news for writers is that we're already very good at this. That's what we do. We understand people and we seek to help or entertain them.

At least that's what most writers do. The good ones. But this is good news for the not-so-good writers too, because it gives a clear path to get better fast.

We don't have to wonder, what should I be writing about? We don't have to sit in front of our keyboards for hours, writing garbage and *knowing* it's garbage but not really knowing why. Once we figure out it's all about empathy, we can focus on building it, then writing based on it.

This is good news for the editors and marketing managers too. It gives them a clear line and a clear path to getting massive traffic.

But we can't just understand the human condition in a vague sense. To get traffic, we have to get as close to the reader as humanly possible. We have to understand what made him type his search term. We have to know what he felt like inside when he typed it and why. We have to know what's making the searcher's stomach churn or keeping him up at night for *this search query.* We have to get so specific we can almost see his eye color and the small hairs on the back of his wrist.

But How?

We know now that thinking like Google means serving the reader as well as we can. But that's like saying quitting smoking just means not smoking any more. Of course, but how?

Well, that's where all the great and constantly-evolving tools of SEO come roaring in to help. All those tools like keyword research and competitive analysis and link-building and comment-building and everything you've heard about from SEO gurus for years. Until now it may have sounded like a lot of sticky magic. But suddenly it becomes a tool to help you in your quest to figure out what the reader wants and give it to him. It helps *you* see into the heart of every reader, so you can sit and chew your disgusting spring-greens salad or ham sandwich and say, "It'll work!" or "Nobody cares."

Yes, we have to use keywords if we want to rank. We have to do competitive analyses and use all sorts of other SEO tools. But we don't pick up the tools like crusty wizards with arcane knowledge in a Terry Pratchett novel. Because every SEO tool you use, you should *only* use in the service of one thing: delivering what the reader wants.

The rest of this book shows how.

Before we get into specific SEO tools, let's talk for a minute about what the reader wants.

Rand Fishkin called it *searcher task accomplishment* or *search intent.* What problem is the reader trying to solve? Is she trying to learn how to build a birdhouse or figure out how to deal with her son's fever? Is she trying to learn how to get a job working from home or get some tips from other business leaders on how to run her corporation?

In some cases the problem won't have a solution. In a class I taught on SEO, one of my students—a journalist with credits in *The Wall Street Journal, Forbes, CNBC,* and *Bloomberg*—lamented, "But I don't want always to be writing how-to guides. Is that what I'm reduced to if I want to master SEO?

Absolutely not. In some cases the "problem" is the reader is frustrated and wants to be understood, or wants to vent, or wants straight info to counteract a baseless political argument from a friend. Those are still problems. They're just not "how to" problems. In every case, if you want to rank high, you have to understand that the reader has *some* kind of problem and you need to solve it.

Here's a little example. Let's say you search, "I hate my job." Are you looking for a solution? Or are you just at the end of your rope? Chances are, if you've reached the far-out breaking point of crying on Google's shoulder, you don't really expect an answer. You probably just want to feel like you're normal and not alone. You may want to see comments from lots of others who feel the same way, or read about people who were in that situation but made it through to a much better place.

In other words, your "problem" might be that you lack hope.

If that's the case, the best article for you will give you hope. It will likely also give a little advice for what to do about your plight, but hope will be the central theme. The best article will make the reader come away thinking, "I'm okay. Things will be okay."

Writer Michael Tomaszewski did just this when he wrote Google's #1 result for "I hate my job."

He wrote a caring, heartfelt article that feels the reader's pain. It spends a long time giving reasons for exhaustion and cynicism. It acknowledges that the reader is miserable, hopeless, has a terrible boss, and wants to quit.

(Source: Google.com)

The piece does give advice on what to do, but mainly it's a shoulder to cry on. It ranks high not because Tomaszewski understood the reader *doesn't want advice.* Instead, his reader wants to feel okay and understood. Tomaszewski served the searcher by building massive empathy before he wrote a single word.

The rest of the chapters in this book provide tools for figuring out search intent and providing good solutions.

PART 2: HOW TO SEE INTO THE READER'S HEART

CHAPTER 4: USE KEYWORDS TO READ YOUR READER'S MIND

Don't use keywords, he says. Then he tells us to use keywords.

Well, for now, we still have to use keywords. But—

Don't use them like everybody else.

To teach SEO, I could meet you in a classroom and start showing spreadsheets jammed with keywords on an overhead projector. That would be a dry, academic way to teach the basics.

You'd have no reason to listen, other than, "I need to learn this stuff to keep my job."

But now you know better. Already you know keywords aren't about jumping through hoops so Google will acknowledge you. They're not about spreadsheets and proper placement and tricking an heuristic.

Instead, you know SEO is about seeing into the reader's heart.

In chapter 1, I referenced those fantastic editors of yesteryear. They were savants at empathy. Later, they were replaced by online editors. Now Google itself has usurped their function.

But Google doesn't write the articles. It doesn't even pick them. It just sets up a system that lets *readers* pick the articles.

So who's the empathy savant now?

It's you.

But I'm not a genius at empathy. And I don't chew anything disgusting.

Here's the good news: you don't have to be.

With SEO tools like keyword research, competitive analysis, social media analysis, and others in this book, you can build that powerful, traffic-getting empathy through craft. It takes a little elbow-grease. But, to coin a spoonerism, "It ain't rocket surgery." And once you've done it a few times, it will:

1. Become second nature
2. Make your actual writing *a lot* faster.

The first tool we'll cover is keyword research. I put it on an equal footing with several others, but it makes sense to talk about keywords first because they're so misunderstood.

The key point here? Keywords aren't SEO. They won't teleport you to the top ranking spot in Google. So dial down your enthusiasm for them by about 90%.

All they'll do is help you glimpse the searcher's thoughts. That's powerful, but it's not a magic bullet.

So—if you want to use keywords to see into your reader's heart so you can rank, where do you start?

By picking a focus keyword.

What's a Focus Keyword?

Picture this:

You write the coolest article ever. You're so proud of it. You do some great research, add mind-blowing quotes from super-famous people, write it, and put it on the internet.

You're going to get a million views!

Except—crickets. Nobody reads it, including your mom.

If you're a writer and you're confused about SEO, you don't have to picture it. It happens every day.

Well, the first part of the solution is to pick a focus keyword.

That's just the main keyword you want your article to rank for. Are you writing an article about the different uses of orange oil? Well then "orange oil uses" is probably your focus keyword.

Is your article about the highest earning hedge fund managers? Then "highest earning hedge fund managers" is your focus keyword.

Sounds basic, but it's a step a lot of writers fail to think about. Doing it right is the first step toward knowing where your reader is coming from.

How to Pick a Focus Keyword

Here's the good news:

Picking a focus keyword is simple. You just:

1. Pick one with a lot of search traffic.
2. That's it.

Lots of search traffic means bigger problems that vex more people. That gives you a bigger empathy account. But how can you know if your focus keyword has a lot of traffic?

With a keyword research tool.

Keyword Research Tools

I know—ugh. Keyword research. Pass me the slide rule, will you Horace? Let me bust out my best Jerry Lewis accent from *The Nutty Professor.*

No, we won't do that. Remember, keywords are about empathy, and that's the only way we'll use them.

So, which keyword tool should you use?

There are several. Take your pick. I'll use ahrefs, because it's popular and works well, but here's a quick list of the top contenders:

- **Moz.** Created by SEO gurus Rand Fishkin and Gillian Meussig in 2004. $99/mo. 30-day free trial.
- **Ahrefs.** A multinational keyword research tool started in 2011. $99/mo. 7-day trial for $7.
- **SEMRush.** A global keyword research and online marketing research tool. $99/mo. 7-day free trial. 10 free searches/day.
- **Wordtracker.** $27 a month and fairly well-respected. 10 free searches a day. 7-day free trial.

These are the cream of the crop. There are others, but since this book isn't a piece of 10x content, I'll stick with these.

Now let's look at how to use a keyword tool to build reader empathy.

Use Ahrefs to See Your Reader's Thoughts

Here was my horror:

When I first started doing keyword research, I thought, *I'm already strapped for time. Now I've got to do hours of keyword research before I write?*

Well, no.

The process I'm about to describe looks involved. In fact, the first time through, it *is* involved, because you've got to familiarize yourself with some new tools.

But after a bit you'll do it in about five minutes.

Step 1:

Come up with a topic you want to write about, then plug it into a keyword research tool. The tool spits back a list of related words. It shows how many people search for each word every month.

Here's an example using the ahrefs keyword explorer tool.

Let's say you're writing an article about how to invest in real estate. You go to the Ahrefs Keyword Explorer Tool and type, "invest in real estate." Here's what pops up:

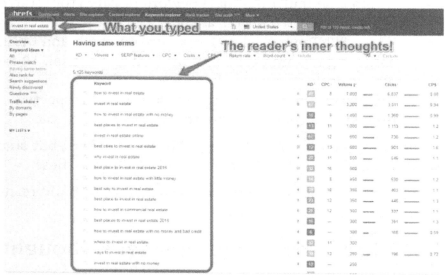

You just hit paydirt. Look at these related terms:

- How to invest in real estate
- How to invest in real estate with no money
- Invest in real estate online
- Why invest in real estate
- Best way to invest in real estate
- Best places to invest in real estate
- How to invest in commercial real estate
- Ways to invest in real estate

To broaden things, I varied the term a little bit to "real estate investing" and searched again:

- Real estate articles
- Real estate investing for beginners
- How to get into real estate investing

- Real estate investing courses
- Real estate investors near me
- Getting started in real estate investing

This is gold. The searcher who looks for "invest in real estate" is a newbie. (We'll call her Alice. Nice Zappos, Alice.) She really wants to invest in real estate but doesn't know an appraisal from a closing cost.

How should she start? What articles should she read? What are the pitfalls, rookie mistakes, and top-line tips? Are there classes she should take? What about networking? Are there LinkedIn groups or local meetups she should know about?

This kind of keyword research isn't data crunching. It isn't trying to fool an algorithm into ranking you. It's a sneaky way to read your reader's thoughts. This very minor, 1-minute keyword research gives you a mini qualifying conversation with your reader.

Here's another useful tidbit: the keyword list you got from ahrefs is organized by search volume. It shows that 16,280 people look for "real estate investing" every month. Meanwhile, 7,800 search for "how to invest in real estate," and only 500 search "real estate investors near me."

So, we can prioritize our list. We know which terms are more important and which the reader only sort of cares about. That gives us a valuable clue for outlining our article. We may want to put higher-traffic terms first. That way, Alice will see at a glance that we've given her the most valuable info right away. She'll stick with our article longer. Google will see that and grant boons a'plenty.

Where Do Those Traffic Estimates Come From?

To quote a guy who used to call in to the local rock station I worked at, after news breaks:

"Where do you get your information?!"

Ahrefs' traffic estimates come from Google Keyword Planner, augmented by data from browser apps and plugins.

The other tools I mentioned do the same. After years of writing high-ranking articles, then comparing my traffic to their estimates, I can say they're fairly accurate.

But Wait, There's More

A tiny amount of keyword research can give you a window into your reader's mind. But it's not the only way.

Sometimes you won't find a lot of data in ahrefs. (In that case you might have a dud topic nobody cares about—but more on that later.)

Once I had to write a piece on the best resume writers in NYC. I know, where's my Pulitzer, right? My quick keyword research showed a lot of terms like:

- Professional resume writer New York City
- Best resume writer New York City
- Good resume writer New York City
- And you get the idea.

No amazing insights.

If that happens (and it will) you're not out of keyword ammo yet. You can crack into PAA and LSI for clues.

Find Reader Frustrations With PAA

PAA is short for "People Also Ask." It's ridiculously simple to use once you know how.

Just Google-search your topic, then scroll to the bottom of the first page of results. You'll see a little list like this:

Searches related to invest in real estate

how to invest in real estate with little money   cheapest way to invest in real estate

how to invest in real estate book   real estate investment groups

invest in real estate online   investing in real estate rentals

real estate investing for beginners   real estate investing app

1 2 3 4 5 6 7 8 9 10   Next

(Source: Google.com)

Look familiar? You get one free with every search. It helps because it shows questions your reader isn't finding answers to. Sometimes Google puts it at the top, and sometimes they call it, "related searches."

By any name, it gives more clues to your reader. She may be interested in rentals or investing in real estate online. (Is that possible? I'd better research it!) She might be curious about real estate investment groups. Apps, too. (Hey! I didn't know they had real estate investment apps. I'll look into them.)

As you're spotting all these things, you're not just thinking, "Hmm. That's interesting." Instead, you'll cleverly open a Google Doc, Word document, or spreadsheet and populate it with your findings, thus:

ahrefs	PAA
How to invest in real estate	Real estate rental investment
Real estate articles	Real estate online investing
Real estate investing for beginners	Real estate investment groups
How to invest with no money	Real estate investment apps
How to get into real es-	

tate investing	
Real estate investing courses	
Real estate investors near me	
Getting started in real estate investing	
Best way to invest in real estate	

These terms will be gold when you start to outline.

Spackle in the Gaps With LSI

Keywords can still show us a little more about our reader's problem. Our last keyword tool is LSI.

That stands for Latent Semantic Indexing. It's a technique from the 80s that finds the latent (hidden) relationships between words. So if I say "winter," the word "weather" is related. So are "boots" and "wonderland." Those are obvious, but lots of LSI matches aren't.

For years, SEO experts thought LSI was the key to ranking high. They were confident Google used it to see if you had the right related words on your page.

Most SEO pros now think that was a blind alley. If Google ever used LSI, they've long since mothballed it in favor of machine learning tactics like the ones I described in earlier chapters.

So why am I telling you about it?

Because LSI *can* help. Not to trick Google, but (again) to look into your reader's mind.

Here's how:

You pop over to a free online LSI generator to grab a list of LSI terms. You type in "real estate invest." The site kicks back a list.

Usually it's pretty long. I've shortened this one for clarity. I've also put new terms we haven't come across yet in bold:

- real estate investing for beginners
- real estate investment groups
- real estate investing app
- **types of real estate investment**
- real estate investing companies
- real estate investing books
- **real estate investment trust**
- how to invest in real estate with little money
- real estate investing for beginners books
- investing in real estate rentals
- top real estate investment groups
- real estate investment companies
- how to find real estate investors in your area
- **crowdfunding real estate**
- real estate investing app 2018
- best apps for real estate investors 2018
- **SHA**

You've probably noticed many of those terms were also in our ahrefs search. (Hmm. Maybe ahrefs uses LSI to generate their keywords?) But—

There are a few key differences: *types of real estate, real estate investment trust, crowdfunding real estate,* and *SHA (loans).*

Could your reader be curious about them? Maybe. Add them to the third column of your keyword spreadsheet, like this:

ahrefs	PAA	LSI
How to invest in real estate	Real estate rental investment	types of real estate
Real estate articles	Real estate online investing	real estate investment trust
Real estate investing for beginners	Real estate investment groups	crowdfunding real estate
How to invest	Real estate invest-	SHA

with no money	ment apps	
How to get into real estate investing		
Real estate invest- ing courses		
Real estate in- vestors near me		
Getting started in real estate investing		
Best way to invest in real estate		

Now you've got a robust batch of keywords. They provide a peek into the reader's thoughts. They won't write your article for you or drop a silver bullet in your lap. They're worth the 5–10 minutes you'll spend doing this for each article you write.

A Word About the Yoast Plugin

If you've written articles in WordPress, you've probably seen the Yoast plugin.

Yoast is the brainchild of SEO whiz Joost de Valk. It tells if your content is likely to rank high.

When you write a piece in WordPress, Yoast asks for a focus keyword, SEO title, and other odds and ends. Then it gives feedback that looks like this:

- The focus keyword doesn't appear in the first paragraph of the copy. Make sure the topic is clear immediately.

- No internal links appear in this page, consider adding some as appropriate.

- This page has 0 nofollowed outbound link(s) and 46 normal outbound link(s).

- The keyword density is 0.9%, which is great; the focus keyword was found 31 times.

- The meta description contains the focus keyword.

- The meta description has a nice length.

- The focus keyword appears only in 5 (out of 22) subheadings in your copy. Try to use it in at least one more subheading.

- The images on this page contain alt attributes with the focus keyword.

- The text contains 3547 words. This is more than or equal to the recommended minimum of 300 words.

- The SEO title contains the focus keyword, at the beginning which is considered to improve rankings.

- The SEO title has a nice length.

- The focus keyword appears in the URL for this page.

Yoast wants you to put the focus keyword in your copy between 0.5% and 3% of the time. Notice in the image above, Yoast says my focus keyword density was 0.9%. It likes that.

Should you worry about this stuff?

I've always found the Yoast plugin vaguely helpful. If you're a beginner, it can keep you on track. It can make sure you don't do things to make Google angry, like keyword stuffing or slapping in too many internal links.

But—take it with a grain of salt.

For example, in a 3,000 word post, if the focus keyword shows up 30 times, that's reasonable.

But here's the thing: Google doesn't like you thinking about it that way. To Google, using an algorithm to satisfy its algorithm is barking up the wrong tree.

As Google relies less and less on keywords, you should too. There are even articles out there these days that rank for terms *not even in the article.*

It's better to think of it like this:

If you write a really good 3,000 word article about lawn sprinklers, the term "lawn sprinklers" will probably show up about 30 times naturally anyway. If it shows up 90 times, you're either stuffing keywords or you have a small vocabulary.

When I'm done writing a piece, I go back to my keyword research spreadsheet and look at it again. I check to see if my focus keyword is spread throughout my piece about 1% of the time. I check to see if the other terms in my spreadsheet show up here and there. If they don't, maybe I've missed a point I should've covered—for the reader's sake.

But I never try to stuff more keywords in for Google's sake.

The bottom line? Use Yoast to keep from going overboard and making Google angry. But always come back to the reader's needs. Keep those as true North, and you won't go wrong.

One side note about editors:

The reality is that many of them will make content creators shoehorn keywords into their copy. That works but in my opinion it isn't future-proof unless it's done in a very natural way.

When you've got a choice between writing and awkward sentence and leaving out your keyword, cut the keyword.

Pulling it All Together

Should you try to write an article that bundles in all the terms and topics in your keyword research?

Probably not. Unless you're writing a 10x article called *The*

Ultimate Guide to Real Estate Investing for Beginners, you shouldn't slavishly dump all these phrases into it.

But if you're targeting "real estate investing" pay attention to them, because your reader cares about them. If those sentence fragments are your reader's thoughts, what does it say about her? About her needs?

Going through these steps with ahrefs, PAA, and LSI will make your pieces stronger because you'll be more focused on what your reader cares about.

You're starting to build a mental picture of her. Of what's keeping her up at night and making her stomach churn. If you take five minutes to follow these steps before you outline, the right words will show up naturally in the right places in your article. But the real win will be that Alice reads it and thinks, "This writer read my mind!"

That's thinking like Google.

Learn to do it, and people will spend more time in your articles. As a nice side bonus, Google will float your work higher in the rankings.

At bottom, keyword research is just a 5–10 minute exercise in mocking up a mini-conversation with the reader. But it's far from the whole story. We also need to know how our reader feels and how she talks about it. But first we need to understand how to choose our battles.

CHAPTER 5: PICK TOPICS THAT START A TRAFFIC-LANCHE

Let's take a big step backwards.

I just showed you how to spend 5–10 minutes learning your reader's thoughts with keyword research. I'm dying to tell you how to do it even better with a few more tools.

But what if your topic—frankly—sucks?

You could spend 20 minutes putting on your reader's shoes, then four hours writing a fantastic article. But then—

Chirp, chirp, chirp.

Three people read it. One is your Aunt Hazel. She sends you a long email saying what a great writer you are. You don't tell her you're a fraud because you don't want to break her special heart. Instead, you give a peppy, "Thanks, Aunt Hazel!" and change the subject so fast you singe your fingers.

Why didn't you get traffic? You wrote a great article, right? You satisfied the reader!

Maybe you ranked #1 in Google but *still* didn't get traffic. (Hint: nobody was searching for your topic. "How to use sphagnum to improve your IQ" might work on social media, but not for SEO.)

Or maybe you wrote the best and brightest article *ever*, but you still landed on page 50.

Either way, what went wrong?

You probably jumped into keyword research before you thought about the topic.

Let's look back at the example in the last chapter.

I picked, "real estate invest." Seems likely. But what would happen if we actually wrote an article about it?

Let's find out. While we're at it, let's look at how to pick topics that set us up for success. It's not hard. It's fast. But if you do it, your keyword research will make *a lot more sense* and you'll increase your chance of getting traffic exponentially.

So, as Jeff Goldblum says in *Thor Ragnarok,* "without further adieu," here's a 4-step plan to pick topics that unleash a traffic-lanche.

1. Check What's Succeeding Now

Let's take the focus keyword, "real estate invest." How can we know if it's a dud?

The first thing we'll do is Google it:

(Source: Google.com)

Google gave us four ads, an image, and a "featured snippet" of text on the right side with a little info about investment trusts.

It also showed ten articles. They're all geared toward beginners. Most are how-to-get-started guides. If we click them, we see they're not massive, 10,000-word posts. Most are 1,500–2,000 words.

They're well-presented. They're hosted on respected sites like Forbes and BiggerPockets. That gives us a clue. There's traffic to be had here (or those big publications wouldn't target the term).

From that quick look at existing articles, I know:

1. It won't take a week to write my version.
2. There's enough traffic to make it worth my while.
3. My reader is a beginner who wants basic info.

That's great! I'm way ahead of where I was.

But can I compete?

2. Pick Your Battles

Have you ever written a great article that completely failed to rank? Maybe it appeared on page four, but never climbed from there?

If not, you haven't been at this very long. Either that or you're some kind of SEO magician. (Call me and let's talk.)

A big part of why we don't rank is sometimes that we haven't learned to pick our battles.

Sometimes as a writer, you're given topics from on high. If so, you're stuck. However, if you have *any* say in what you write about, do a little checking first to make sure you're surfing a wave—not storming a well-defended beach-head.

Where You Work Matters

Are you creating content for *Forbes* or for *Jimmy Bob's Business and Meat Snack Blog*? It pays to know the difference.

Each site has a *Domain Authority* (DA). That's not an official Google term. It's a search engine ranking score developed by Moz. It predicts how well a page will rank, based on how much Google (probably) respects it. *Forbes* has a Domain Authority of 95 (out of 100) and *Jimmy Bob's* probably has a DA of 3.

The higher your Domain Authority, the more Google respects you, and the easier it is to rank. That's why a 300-word nothing-article in Forbes will sometimes outrank a perfect 2,000-word post in a no-name publication. (Though Google seems to be changing this.)

How does Moz calculate Domain Authority? They look at how many links a site gets from other well-respected sites. If CNN, the BBC, and Harvard all link to you, you probably did something very right.

How can you use this?

1. Check your site's Domain Authority by typing your URL into Moz's Link Explorer.
2. Check who's dominating your topic by Googling it.
3. Check *their* Domain Authority (DA).
4. Compare your DA to their DA.
5. If the two DAs are close, there's a good chance you can compete.

For instance, let's say we check our topic, and *Forbes* is #1 for it. So we go to Moz and check Forbes' Domain Authority and see it has a score of 95.

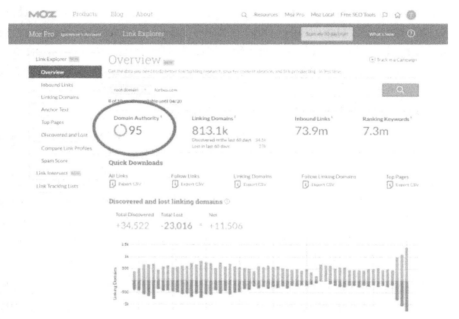

Meanwhile, we're writing articles for Jimmy Bob, with a DA score of 3.

You could say we don't have a snowflake's chance in a blast furnace of beating Forbes no matter how great a job we do connecting to the reader.

It's easy to know this with sites like Forbes *without* checking Domain Authority. But checking DA comes in handy with sites you're less familiar with.

How much time does this take? Too much. copy-pasting ᴉ0 URLs into a DA checker for every topic you research takes *forever.*

Luckily the MozBar plugin for Google Chrome makes this process lightning-fast. With the plugin, you don't have to copy-paste a lot of URLs every time you test a topic.

When you do a Google search, the MozBar shows DA for every result. It also shows PA (Page Authority—same as Domain Authority, but for the specific page instead of the whole site). Then it shows the number of links in to the page.

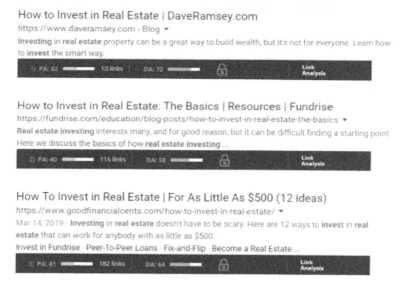

(Source: Google.com)

Now if I'm creating content for a site with a DA of 30, I can look at those results and see I've got a fair shot at getting in. The best part? You don't have to pay a penny for it.

How Much Does Domain Authority Matter?

The good news? Domain authority doesn't matter as much as

it used to. I think the big brains who work at Google started asking, "Why are we ranking garbage from the bigwigs higher than excellent posts from the little guys?"

So, in one update or another, Google dialed down the Moxie on Domain Authority. That's great news for content marketers, because it democratizes things. Write the best page, and you've got a shot at getting in, even if the big boys dominate the topic.

Now you know how to check if you can compete. Next, let's learn to find the places you can really soar.

Find Gaps in the Web

The web is full of holes. That's not a Zen koan or a Beatles lyric. There are actually topics nobody's written good articles about. The golden formula is:

1. The topic has weak content.
2. The sites serving it have low Domain Authority.

Create content for those topics, and you'll rank easily. Find gaps like that with lots of traffic, and you've struck a hidden vein of internet gold.

At the money site I worked at, we weren't getting any traffic at first. Then an insider at Google told the owner, "net worth articles are underserved." So, I did real research, wrote long, well-presented net worth articles, and ranked easily.

It's nice if you've got inside info from Google. If you don't, you can still find good gaps on your own.

Here's how:

1. Find Your Competition

Log into SEMRush or Ahrefs again. This time, instead of typing a keyword, type your site's URL.

A few years ago I got hired by a medical waste website to raise their traffic from 8,000 views a month to 45,000 in three months. They had a DA of 32. They weren't starting from scratch, but they weren't heavy hitters, either.

So—I logged into SEMRush, typed their URL, and got a list of 8,022 competitors:

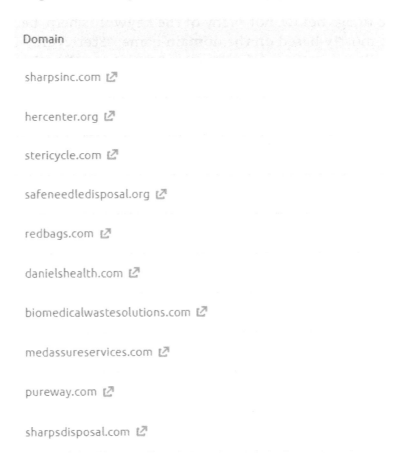

Organic Competitors 1 - 100 (8,022) *i*

Domain

sharpsinc.com

hercenter.org

stericycle.com

safeneedledisposal.org

redbags.com

danielshealth.com

biomedicalwastesolutions.com

medassureservices.com

pureway.com

sharpsdisposal.com

(Source: SEMRush.com)

Why did I do this? I wanted to find out where all the traffic was.

2. Find Your Competition's Highest-Traffic Keywords

Once you know who you're competing with, take a look at where they're getting traffic.

To do it, click their URL in SEMRush (or Ahrefs).

I did this for my medical waste client's top 100 competitors and got a list of each site's highest-traffic keywords. Holy cow, right? What a goldmine!

In the image below, not many of the keywords help, because they're mostly based on the domain name, "Stericycle." But a couple like "sharps container" and "a&d ointment" look promising.

Organic Search Positions 1 - 100 (41,370) _i_

	Keyword	Pos.	Diff.	Traffic	Traffic %
>	stericycle	1 → 1	0	26,480	50.78
>	mystericycle	1 → 1	0	2,320	4.44
>	stericycle jobs	1 → 1	0	1,280	2.45
>	stericycle indianapolis	1 → 1	0	1,040	1.99
>	stericycle careers	1 → 1	0	1,040	1.99
>	stericycle inc	1 → 1	0	800	1.53
>	sharps container	3 → 3	0	729	1.39
>	mystericycle com	1 → 1	0	704	1.35
>	a&d ointment	11 → 11	0	695	1.33
>	stericycle login	1 → 1	0	576	1.10

(Source: SEMRush.com)

I did this for 100 sites, and built a spreadsheet of keywords with at least 1,000 searches a month. I wound up with a list of about 500 high-traffic keywords in the industry.

3. Find Out Where You Can Compete

Once you know your competition and their highest traffic-earning keywords, see if there are soft spots in the list. Places with bad content or low Domain Authority competitors.

To do it, Google each keyword on your list. Use the Moz plugin to see the DA of the top contenders. If they're all much higher than your site's DA, consider walking away. If not, you've found a soft spot. Pop it in a spreadsheet of good focus keywords and move on.

I did this for my med waste client and found out:

1. What are the top 500 traffic-earning keywords in the medical waste world?
2. Which ones have the weakest competition?

4. Write Content

Once you've got your list of internet soft spots with high traffic, start writing content. This is where you go back to your 5–10 minutes of quick keyword research to understand your reader's thoughts.

I did that for 40 days for my medical client, writing a new 2,200-word article every day around each of my top 35 terms. My highest-traffic keyword had about 10,000 monthly views. My lowest had 1,000. By day 35, I hit the goal of 45,000 visits a month.

Don't Run From Glory

Here's the problem with picking topics based only on Domain Authority:

If you do it, you'll be always chasing after scraps.

It's easy to rank for internet soft spots.

It's also a breeze to win in topic areas you already dominate.

For the money site, my first net worth article took three

months to get to #1. But soon, my new net worth pieces would hit the top spot in a couple days.

Then I switched to articles like, "how much money do people make for an Oscar?" or "for winning Wimbledon?" or "for playing in the NFL?" Again, my first piece like that took months to rank, but after a few successes, I could rank high fast.

Sticking with your strengths is great, but if you never take on the big contenders, you'll never break out of scavenger-mode.

If you're selling watches, you can't avoid topics like "best watches" because of scary competition. Pick your battles, yes, but don't run from a fight. I was shocked at first when I started outranking Forbes and Fortune with my own tiny DA of 25, but I did it. It's harder to take down the behemoths, but if you serve the reader well enough, you will.

For example, at Zety.com, we weren't guaranteed to rank when we started writing resume guides. But we're a Software-as-a-Service (SaaS) site that sells an online resume builder. We couldn't walk away from resume guides because of heavy competition.

So, we wrote a *lot* of resume guides and cross-linked them. We also wrote the best guides on the market. Doing that comes down to solid keyword research, but you also have to *know* the market. You can't just pick high-traffic topics and know your reader's surface thoughts. You also have to have some way to serve the reader's needs. That's up next.

CHAPTER 6: BUILD EMPATHY WITH COMPETITIVE ANALYSIS

We've still got a major problem.

Let's say you picked a good topic that gets a pile of monthly traffic, and you know you can compete. (Or, you can't, but you need to roll up your sleeves and attack the topic anyway.)

Either way, your 5–10 minute keyword research has given you a glimpse into the reader's thoughts. The reader—Alice—has a problem, and you feel it.

But:

1. You don't *fully* understand it. Not enough to write the article.
2. You don't know how to *solve* it. You can't give good advice.

This is where competitive analysis comes in.

Here's how to do it right:

1. Google Your Keyword

Keyword research is nice, but it doesn't paint the whole picture. If you write content based on keyword insights alone, you'll have to reinvent the wheel. And it'll probably be square.

To feel our reader's pain more, Google-search your focus keyword and check the top-ranked articles.

What problem do they solve for the reader? How do they do it? What advice do they give? What's their style? Do they use lots of images and videos? Who are they geared toward? Is there a gender angle?

The point is not to reverse-engineer these articles. Saying the same thing as everybody else doesn't serve the reader. If Alice already has ten orange popsicles, does she really need another?

The point is to figure why those top-ranked articles are winning. Doing that will help us build a better mental image of the reader. Then we'll figure how to do it better.

2. See What's Already Winning and Why

How can you help Alice if you don't know what help she's already getting?

You can't sell her a pen unless you know if she already has one, right?

So, we'll start with the top result in Google. It's "How to Invest in Real Estate," on DaveRamsey.com. We'll jot down the page's understanding of the reader's problem. Then we'll add any bits of useful info or advice, like this:

- How to Invest in Real Estate—daveramsey.com
  - Problem
    - R.E. investing seems like a great idea, but it's a big commitment and most don't understand it.
  - Advice & Key Points
    - Types of R.E. investing (rentals, house-flipping, trusts).
    - House flipping takes time and patience.
    - Rental income gives quicker income but is

time-consuming.

- ■ Taxes can be complex (capital gains, rental income).
- ■ A six-step plan for how to invest.
- ■ Wait until you've paid off your home first.

This Dave Ramsey piece is Google's favorite page for the "real estate invest" keyword. Remember, that means it's also the reader's favorite page. So Ramsey is obviously doing something right.

His page is even beating several others that have much higher PA/DA scores. But why?

Maybe readers just love Dave Ramsey. He's a popular public figure in the money world. But maybe the article really "gets" the reader's problem and serves the best solutions.

Now let's add to our bullet list by skimming the other articles and picking up tidbits—shown in bold:

- ● Dave Ramsey (plus the other top 10 articles)
  - ○ Problem
    - ■ R.E. investing seems like a great idea, but it's a big commitment and most don't understand it. **Also it can be scary and risky. Huge, tempting returns, but we don't want to lose our shirts. There's lots of predators out there.**
  - ○ Advice & Key Points
    - ■ Types of R.E. investing (rentals, house-flipping, trusts, **Airbnb, funds, online investing, commercial, ETFs).**
    - ■ House flipping takes time and patience.
    - ■ Rental income gives quicker income but is time-consuming.
    - ■ Taxes can be complex (capital gains, rental income).
    - ■ A six-step plan for how to invest.

- Wait until you've paid off your home first.
- **How to do it with a day job**
- **How to do it with no money**
- *How to dodge the predators*

I added that last bullet myself because it occurred to me that nobody in the top 10 answered it.

So—that's a snapshot of all the info in the top 10 articles in Google for "real estate invest." Most of it repeats a lot, but some articles have a fresh nugget here or there.

Technically, if we wanted to write the best article on the web about this topic, we could just use the list above as our new outline. We'd improve on Ramsey's #1 article by adding bonus material from others. But something tells me we still wouldn't rank.

3. Fill in Your Picture of the Reader

Something's missing. Can you feel it? If we write our article now, we're signing up for a lot of work and a weak chance at scoring high.

What's wrong?

We've got a good topic. We've got our keyword research spreadsheet from chapter four. Adding my competitive analysis, I can tell several things about the reader. First, she's really tempted by the big money she could make from real estate. But she's also worried—with good reason.

She's interested in the different types of real estate income. (I was pretty jazzed up about the Airbnb idea myself.)

She likes reading about the dangers and the steps to get around them. She's curious about investing with no money and a day job.

But now it's time to sit back and do a little head-scratching to find a way to serve Alice a *lot* better than the others.

When I get to this part I ask myself, is there some way to deliver all this info in a cleaner way? Could I write a more gripping introduction? Could I share better resources with Alice? Books? Articles? Videos?

The top ten articles are almost always missing *something*. Maybe they take too long to get to the point. Or they ramble. Or they don't present the information in the cleanest way. Or they miss the forest for the trees.

Two Examples

How can you make competitive analysis work for you?

Let me give you two examples.

When I was working at the money site, I decided to write an article about how much money NFL referees make. Football season was in full swing, and I'd noticed my articles around pigskin topics gaining traffic.

So I Googled "NFL referee money." Every article in the top 10 said referees make $173,000 a year. I was tempted to write my article using that same number, but I wanted to serve the reader better.

So, I started digging into the statistic. Where did it come from? Article #1 in Google's lineup didn't say where it got the number. Neither did the second. The third cited the fourth. The fourth cited the fifth. They all had the same piece of information, but I couldn't verify it or trace the source.

Finally, one of the articles cited a 2012 report from the NFL that set the *average NFL salary for all officials* at $173,000 in 2013. Adjusting for a historical raise amount of 2.87% per year, that number would hit $188,000 by 2016. So already, $173,000 wasn't right. But here's the bigger issue:

All *officials* are not *referees.* An official can be a line judge, back judge, side judge, field judge, replay official, or yes, a referee. Referees are special, manager-level officials who lead all the others.

So, was it likely that referees earned the average salary of *all* officials? That would be like saying restaurant managers make minimum wage because the average restaurant employee earns that much.

I wrote my article around that, adding my reverse-engineered estimate of $500,000 a year. I showed my work on that estimate to show the reader why it made sense. The article almost instantly popped up at #1 in Google. It won dozens of links, including one from *Bleacher Report*. It became one of our top traffic earners for over a year.

Why? Because I wasn't parroting. I was giving Alice something no one else could give her.

This was kind of an, "If you build it, they will come" moment for me. I'd made a better mousetrap. It worked, but it had nothing to do with keyword placement and everything to do with serving the reader better than anybody else. In a sea of cookie-cutter content, if you can convince the reader fast that you've got something different and more valuable, you've won.

My second example is an article I wrote about prize money in the US Open tennis championship. I knew I wanted to write the article, but I was up against the US Open's website, Wikipedia, CNBC, USA Today, and other gargantuans in the field. How did I rank #1?

I did my competitive analysis and noticed something. Every page gave the same info. The US Open reserved a certain amount of money for its winners in different groups, like singles, doubles, men, and women. There were also different purses if you won Finals, Semifinals, Quarterfinals, etc.

The info was good. It came straight from the US Open's website, and everyone else just copy-pasted it.

I couldn't rank by parroting the same old info freely available on every site. I'd be an also-ran. The readers wouldn't benefit. Google would shunt me to page 1 billion.

So I kept skimming the articles and noodling around and trying to find a wedge.

Then suddenly it hit me.

The numbers were confusing. Try to figure out who wins what and you soon found yourself in a maze of circular logic. I was frowning so hard my eyebrows hurt. Then I realized my reader was doing the same thing. Unless I'd suffered a minor stroke and didn't realize it, you'd have to be a math genius to figure out the money breakdown by reading any of these articles.

So I opened a new spreadsheet and started trying to figure out how the prizes worked. I won't go into it here (thank me with cheeseburgers) but I was able to take the info from mystifying to pretty simple.

I started my intro with the reader's problem: "US Open prize money is really confusing." Then I made an easy-reading table that explained the money situation. I added a few colored charts to make things even simpler, then explained everything with words for readers who wanted to drill deeper.

The article was a success. With our low DA (I think it was about 30 by that point) I beat the pants off sites with DAs of 80, 90, and even 98. My article hit #1 in days. During the US Open, we scored a metric ton of traffic.

Again, it wasn't because I'd stuffed in the right keywords. It was because I took time to dig up the reader's problem. Then I sifted through the competition to see what it did right and where it failed. Finally, I scratched my head and thought of a way to do it better.

There's nothing magic about that process. Most writers, editors, and content creators are natural-born critics anyway. We can skim five articles and quickly tell you why none of them are good.

So—why wouldn't we be able to figure out a way to do it better?

A big part of figuring out the reader's problem is seeing which parts the internet is already solving—and which parts it isn't.

How Long Does It Take?

Do you have to spend a year analyzing the competition for every article you write?

Remember, competitive analysis is:

1. Building a clearer picture of the reader's needs.
2. Looking for a way to fill them better than the rest.

Sometimes you'll find better information. Sometimes you'll say it in a less confusing way.

I know it seems like an awful lot of extra work. But the keyword research and competitive analysis together should take about 10–20 minutes if you don't get bogged down watching embedded cat videos.

The head-scratching and coming up with ways to do things better can take longer. In general, I don't spend more than 40 minutes going through the entire process for any article I write. In most cases I do it a lot faster.

A Case Study in Failure

Sometimes you do everything right and still get your butt kicked.

About a year ago, Zety asked me to write a resume guide for software engineers. They do my keyword research for me—a nice perk of working for a client who "gets" SEO. I did my competitive analysis. I understood the reader's plight.

I wrote a great guide, using several other tools from later

chapters. Soon my article popped up at #1. I had fun reading emails from software engineer friends who stumbled across my advice and reached out to say hello.

Then—disaster. A year later, two other articles outranked me. Why? They did a better job understanding and solving the reader's problem.

The first article that beat me is from KickResume. It's actually not an article at all. It's a gallery of images of about 100 tech resumes the company made for clients. Under each image is a little note like, "Hired by Google," or "Hired by Oracle."

If you click on any of the images, you get a larger view of the resume, with a button that says, "Use sample as my first draft."

It's ingenious. The page assumes the reader:

1. Doesn't want advice.
2. Doesn't want to read anything
3. Wants a good-looking, proven-to-work resume right now, with minimal work.

That's it! It's brilliant. That's why it works. It serves the searcher a million times better than my super-helpful 3,000-word post.

It's also got keywords. Sneaky keywords. But not as many as you'd think. Each image has a title like "IT analyst resume example" or "QA engineer resume example." Not exactly the right keywords—*if* you still believe those are important.

The Final Coffin Nail in Keywords

Need one more piece of evidence it's all about search intent and not keywords? Here it is:

The other guide that burned me serves search intent like nobody's business.

It starts with a sample resume. A really good one.

Then it says, "This is a real resume. It got me tons of interviews at Google, Facebook, Amazon, Microsoft, and Apple."

It says it got those interviews through the black hole of online applications.

Then it explains how the resume works, bit by bit, with tons of actionable advice for how to do it right yourself.

It's an absolutely brilliant guide, and no wonder it smokes my merely great guide.

But—and here's the show-stopper—the phrase "software engineer resume" doesn't show up in it once.

Not once.

(Source: FreeCodeCamp.com)

And yet it still outranked my page, which has the focus keyword 36 times.

If you had any doubt that Google is leaving keywords by the wayside, I hope they've now completely vanished. I hope you really, really believe me when I tell you keywords are just a way to get to know your reader's plight.

By now you know the real goal is search intent, search inte╲ search intent.

The rest of the chapters in this book will turn you into a super-charged machine at seeing into the reader's heart and serving up a smorgasbord for search intent.

CHAPTER 7: FEEL YOUR READER'S PAIN WITH SOCIAL MEDIA

You've read your reader's thoughts, but what about her feelings?

Let's say you sit down to write an article. You've got your massive mug of coffee and your cute bunny stress-squeezer with the popping eyes.

You've got a great topic with zillions of potential readers. You did 15 minutes of keyword research and competitive analysis, so you know where your reader is coming from and how to help her.

But—disaster.

Your article is weak. It's wooden. It's a hairbrained pile of rehashed tips from other articles and from your keyword list.

It's not helping. It's regurgitation. Worse, some of the articles Google loves come from experts in the field. You're just a lowly content creator.

You start questioning your self-worth. Where did you go wrong in life? Maybe your father was right and you should've got a medical degree. How long until you can stop for lunch? Better yet, how long 'til you can die?

Well, let's not reach for the blister pack of Prilosec just yet.

Your problem is that you lack empathy. I'm not saying you're a sociopath. I'm saying you haven't listened to the reader enough to feel her pain.

What is she *really* struggling with? What's giving her night sweats? What's making her say, "um," when a friend says his kid is sick?

That's where social media's got your back.

Social media is a billion readers crying out in the wilderness. It's heartfelt conversation with the reader in a couple minutes.

Alice, here we come.

We'll start with Reddit, because it's by far the most helpful when it comes to building reader empathy.

Reddit: The Internet's Wailing Wall

Reddit has been called a lot of things. It calls itself "the front page of the internet." It says it's full of "fun stories, pics, memes, and videos just for you." It's also been painted as the internet's sewer and (in a nod to Star Wars) a "wretched hive of scum and villainy." In fact, if you Google "Reddit sucks," you get 71.6 million results, and #1 is an in-depth analysis of that suckery by the Washington Post.

There's even a popular subreddit called "This is Why Reddit Sucks." Reddit will sell anything to make a buck—including pieces of itself. "You hate capitalism? I sell things cheap that help with that." It reminds me of a line from Barbara Kingsolver's book *The Poisonwood Bible:* "The jungle eats itself and lives forever."

Now that we're in the right frame of mind, despite its many failings, Reddit is the best way to dig into your reader's heart and watch it bleed.

Here's how:

Let's say you've got your great high-traffic topic. You've armed yourself with keyword research and competitive analysis. But if you write an article from that, it'll come out antiseptic. Your reader will think, "Maybe this article is talking about me. I can't tell. But it doesn't understand me. It doesn't feel my pain. I'm not nodding eagerly as I read the introduction. So I'll click back to Google."

Google will see that and sink you lower in the search results.

So, don't do that.

Don't write your article until you've steeped yourself in Reddit's sewer.

Step 1? Set a time limit. Trust me, you can spend all day watching your reader wallow in his own self-pity. But you don't need to. I like to limit myself to 20 minutes. Often 10 is plenty. Even that sounds long. But it's so worth it.

To do it, Google-search your topic, plus the word "Reddit," like this:

(Source: Google.com)

Oh boy, you've struck the motherlode. Here's what you'll see if you click through to those results:

1. A lot of questions from people trying to get into real estate investing.
2. Mountains of complaints from failed investors about personal disasters.
3. Warnings to newbies about why they should flee like their khakis are on fire.
4. Gold nuggets of advice from real experts who did things right.

You will *really* build a picture of your reader's inner workings.

Here's how to use it like a champion:

1. Find Trends

As you skim Reddit, look for common themes. What questions pop up most? What complaints recur a lot? Those things should wind up higher in your article.

For example, maybe tons of redditors are whining that you can't make money on real-estate rentals because it's impossible to keep them filled. That's a major issue. Note it down. You can do that in a spreadsheet, but I like to add it to my research bullet list.

Or you might find tons of people asking, "How can I find good tenants? All the ones I get won't pay and party all the time." That's a massive clue you've found a pain point. Save it in your notes.

2. Watch for Good Advice

You'll see a lot of complaining on Reddit. That's because a hefty slice of redditors use it as free therapy. They go and vent there about what really makes them angry. If you're hoping to get into nursing, you'll find plenty of advice not to.

But—amid the gripes, you'll find some seasoned pros who genuinely want to help. For example, I had to write a career article for aspiring medical assistants. From Reddit, I learned you can work that role without a certification, then challenge the test once you've got experience.

That's a massive tip for my readers, but I didn't find it in my other research.

Save those tidbits of advice in your bullet list.

Caveats:

You won't find all your advice on Reddit. For that, use your journalism skills like source outreach and online research. Of course fact-check what you find. Reddit is famous for misinformation. I shudder to think what would happen if someone followed only redditor advice.

3. Look for Turns of Phrase

Don't just look for common problems and advice on Reddit. Look for *how* your reader talks. While researching an article for call-center employees, I found terms like:

- *Inmate in a prison*
- *Crazy turnover*
- *SCREAM into the phone*
- *went nuclear on me*
- *the worst*

I dropped several of those turns of phrase into my article. Why? The more you think like your reader, the more you feel like her. You're building empathy. And if you build it, they will come.

Other Windows Into Reader Pain

For most quick content writing, Reddit satisfies. Sometimes I also check Quora—a straight question-and-answer site. The content there can be a little stiffer, but it's still useful. You can also hunt down specialty forums. For example, once I had to write an article on building a home smokehouse for Better Homes & Gardens. I needed info, pictures, and live sources, so I signed up for an account on SmokingMeatForums.com and got everything I needed.

BuzzSumo: What *Everyone* Is Feeling

If you've never used BuzzSumo, you're about to love it. And it's about to add rocket packs to your SEO skills. (It costs $99 a month, but you can do a few free searches a day, and there's a 7-day free trial.)

To use it to see reader feelings:

1. Go to BuzzSumo.com.

2.   Type your topic in the search bar.

3.   Learn a metric ton about your readers.

BuzzSumo will show the most shared, popular content about your topic on Facebook, Twitter, Pinterest, and Reddit. It's also the articles people link to most.

Why is this earth-shaking?

Because you'll get to peek at the writing your reader loves most. You'll get to ask, "Why *this* angle? Why *this* article?"

So, instead of thinking, "How do I get my article about real estate investing to rank high?" You'll think, "I know I need to serve the reader, and here are 10 real estate investing articles that do that *better than the rest.*"

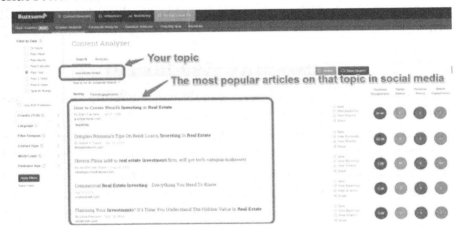

(Source: BuzzSumo.com)

For example, when I click through to #2 in the image above, I get an article about using bank loans to invest in real estate. Seems shady, but I get instant insight into what my reader likes. The article is about a young, successful woman. It packs in lots of Instagram pics of young, smiling, presumably successful people. It's reported interview-style, with a few tips on investing in real estate.

But—

I don't think it's the tips that make the article tick. I think it's the feel. When I read it, I think, wow, that woman is an inspiration. She's so young. She looks like she's got more friends than Jennifer Aniston on Pizza night. She's successful. She makes *me* feel successful just by looking at her.

I think what the article does well is make the reader feel good. Plus, there's a gender theme here. The most-shared articles in the list are either by successful women real estate investors or about them. One is even called, "Females are making it a priority to invest in real estate."

That gives me a Sherlock Holmes-level clue. If I want to rank high with a real-estate investment article, I probably shouldn't picture my reader as a beer-drinking 50-something dude who wants to get into investing with his Wednesday bowling league.

Getting all that intel took me 30 seconds.

Stroke by stroke, we're building up a solid mental image of our reader.

Want more info on how to use BuzzSumo to get your finger on the pulse before you write? Check out this amazing article by the wonderful Sarah Peterson.

While We're at it, Let's Get More Topics

Here's another way to use BuzzSumo to gain reader insight:

Instead of typing in a keyword, type in the URLs of the top blogs in your industry. If you write in the tech space, try techcrunchs.com or pcworld.com. Then look to see what the most shared articles from those sites are.

I just did that and found articles on LG cameras, iPhone headphone jacks, Fallout 76, and Nintendo on the first page of results:

(Source: BuzzSumo.com)

But there are 2,500 other articles in the list. Trolling through them will give me a fantastic birds-eye view of what people in my world are talking about most. That's a goldmine of potential topics.

Use Google Trends to Check Your Work

Don't trust all this keyword and social media research to tell you everything. Some topics are seasonal. They've got a lot of traffic a few days a year. At one site I wrote for, we wrote about topics that had zero traffic and social media interest most days of the year.

That's because we knew they'd spike in certain seasons. We wrote articles about the Super Bowl or the Grammys. We wrote about back-to-school or scholarships. When we checked the Ahrefs data on those terms, we didn't find much. But checking Google Trends told a different story. It showed massive spikes in interest during certain times of year.

Let's say we're writing an article about Peeps. Who doesn't love Peeps, right? Well, me. I can't stand the taste of marshmallow, but I love the idea of them, like coffee or raising twins. But we do our keyword research and we find they don't get a lot of monthly traffic.

But then we peek at Google Trends. Turns out Peeps get a *lot* of traffic once a year. Can you guess when?

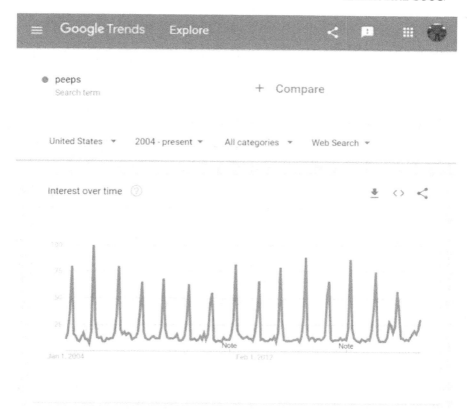

(Source: Google.com)

That gives us a good idea that a topic is worth fighting for, even if the monthly traffic estimates are low most of the year.

The upshot? After you do your keyword and social media research, check Google Trends to make sure you aren't missing something major.

Pulling it All Together

What do we do with all this hash of research? It sounds nice, but how does it really help? And how do we do it quickly, without spending days on it?

Here's how I do it:

1. Keyword research (reader thoughts) 5–10 min

2. Competitive analysis (more thoughts plus advice) 5–10 min
3. Social media analysis (reader feelings) 15–30 min

So, we've got about a half hour to an hour of work before we start to write our piece. That may seem like a lot of time, but we'll make it up on the back end. For example, I coach a couple writers at Zety.com. One of them emailed me today and asked how long it takes me to write a piece.

"I'm finding that it takes me 6–9 hours to write a 1200-word article," he said. "Is that too long?"

My answer was, "it depends." If I already know the material back to front and understand the reader deeply, I can write a piece that long in an hour or two. But if the topic and the searcher are alien to me, a piece that long can take three days.

The point? The time you spend on research pays dividends, slashing twice that much from the time to write the piece. When you understand your reader and her problem, and know how to solve it, writing doesn't take a whole lot longer than talking.

How to Streamline It

One thing that exhausts a lot of writers about SEO research is taming all the data. Copious info about your reader doesn't help if you can't find it while you're writing.

To make things easier, I reduce it to a quick-reference bullet list.

In it, I'll put the top 10 keywords from my keyword research (KR), plus key findings from competitive and social media analysis (CA, SMA). Here's a shortened version for example. (Notice that I've put the monthly traffic estimates near my terms to give them scale.)

- KR

- o How to invest in real estate—7800
- o Real estate articles—1600
- o Real estate investing for beginners—1600
- o How to invest in real estate with no money—1400
- o Real estate investing courses—720
- o Invest in real estate online—600
- o Why invest in real estate—500
- o Best way to invest in real estate—350
- o Real estate investors near me
- **CA**
  - o Problem
    - R.E. investing seems like a great idea, but it's a big commitment and most don't understand it. **Tempting returns but can be scary and risky. Lots of predators.**
  - o Advice & Key Points
    - Types of R.E. investing (rentals, house-flipping, trusts, **Airbnb, funds, online investing, commercial, ETFs).**
    - House flipping takes time and patience.
    - Rental income gives quicker income but is time-consuming.
    - Taxes can be complex (capital gains, rental income).
    - A six-step plan for how to invest.
    - Wait until you've paid off your home.
    - **How to do it with a day job**
    - **How to do it with no money**
    - *How to dodge the predators (my idea)*
- **SMA**
  - o Reddit
    - Can't find good tenants.
    - Can't keep units filled.
    - Airbnb investing is a pain because of cleaning a house every week. If you do it, have a property manager.

- House flipping takes lots of cash and if you don't have cash you don't make profit. You need to find houses selling for much less than they're worth.
- Never get emotionally attached to a property.
- Etc...

o BuzzSumo
- Successful, young, happy women.
- Lots of images of people having fun.
- Positive, confidence-building, pep-talk type stuff works well.

Now we're getting somewhere. That list gives me a deep understanding of my reader. I know who she is and what she wants. I know her hopes and fears. I may not have all the answers, but I can find them now by Googling or reaching out to sources.

In other words, I'm ready to outline my article. For that, I'll use my tried and trusty non-SEO journalism skills.

But it's not enough to build empathy for the reader.

We've also got to convey it. That's up next.

PART 3: SHOW YOU CARE

CHAPTER 8: SHOW THE SEARCHER YOU CARE

Remember the *sell me this pen* sales interview question?

Well, our Keyword Research (KR) Competitive Analysis (CA), and Social Media Analysis (SMA) are our conversation with the searcher. They're the part where we ask, "Do you need a pen? How often do you buy pens? What kinds of pens do you like?"

Now we know the answers to those questions. But the searcher doesn't *know* we know.

We need to show her we've done our homework, and we care.

We'll use several tools to do it. They are:

- Better advice and information than anybody else is giving
- Well-crafted titles and section headings
- Intriguing introductions and opening lines
- Engaging writing
- Examples, images, and videos
- Inviting article structure
- More comments from readers

...and a few more.

I'd love to jump right into explaining them, but there's a problem the size of Google's Berkeley data center that we have to face first.

Here it is:

We already have a giant backhoe that lets us dig into the reader's heart and mind.

It's called an editor. Ignoring it in favor of the other tools can push our noses in.

It Happened to Me

I coach two writers. With my pulse pounding and my tongue out, I taught them all about reader empathy. I got them using KR, CA, and SMA to tap into searcher thoughts and feelings. I helped them write engaging articles with great headlines and other tantalizing bells and whistles.

But one day they both came back and said, "This isn't working."

Editors were rejecting them. Not all, but some. Twenty percent of the editors my writers wrote for didn't like their style.

I said in an earlier chapter that things are changing. I said Google is replacing editors.

Well, let's not throw out the disgusting cigar (or biscotti) with the bathwater. Yes, SEO tools are replacing editor empathy in a big way. But editors are still there to steer the ship, and most do understand their audiences, because they built them.

Your editor may be a savant at empathy still. If not, she may be using the different kinds of research I described in chapters 4–7 to create it.

Maybe she just stockpiled an understanding of her reader over years of publishing lots of articles and reading mounds of letters to the editor. Either way, she has a vision for what works best in her publication.

This is crucial, because it means you have to take the advice in the next few chapters with a huge hunk of pink Himalayan salt.

I'm about to tell you how to write engaging introductions to your articles and sections. I'll show you how to shape massive hooks in your opening lines that keep the reader reading. I'll show how to use examples, images, and pre-existing videos. I'll demonstrate better structure, better advice, and a more pared-down style. All of that will ramp your SEO up to the stratosphere. But—

None of it is any good if the editor can't stand the way you do it. Because if the editor doesn't like those things, you can bet her readers won't appreciate them either.

We still need to know the tools and use them to the best of our ability within the editor's constraints. But the first step to ranking is to understand and work with those constraints.

The "how" of it is simple, and as old as journalism itself.

Find Your Editor's Needs in Her Headlines

It's easy to know what your editor wants.

Just look at what she's already collected.

We talked about picking high-traffic topics in Chapter 5— topics that understand the searcher's needs.

Now we need to refine that to choose topics that also fit our editor's vision of those searcher needs.

To do it:

Look at years of her old headlines. In a print magazine, that means getting hold of a year or two of back issues. The Magzter app is a good way to do that for thousands of popular magazines on less than $10 a month. You can also call the publisher directly or check your local library for print or digital back issues.

I like to type an editor's article headlines into a Google sheet.

As I type, my brain starts generating new ideas that fit her style. I put those in another column.

After I've got ten or so new ideas I think will fit, I'll start pitching them.

With digital publications this is even easier. Just visit the site and start scrolling. One of the writers I coach likes to skim the blogs he likes until he sees a headline that catches his eye. When he finds one, he clicks it and skims it. If he thinks he can do it better, with better advice and a more engaging style, he'll add it to his ideas spreadsheet and pitch it to a similar blog.

Read the Editor's Mind

Success. Your pitch just got accepted. The editor wants you to write the story. Congratulations!

But then—disaster. You write a great article and turn it in, but all you hear is crickets.

This is what happened to the writers I coach. True confession —it also used to happen to me a lot. The editor would love my pitch. I'd write an article that really connected with my reader. Then I'd turn it in and get a cold reception. In one case I even asked, "so did you like it?" The answer was a terse, "Your article has been accepted." Then the article would come out and a huge whack of the words and structure had been changed.

So what went wrong?

The editor and I both had different mental pictures of the reader.

To fix that, I now do a little calibrating to the editor's needs before I write. It's actually pretty easy. I just look through the publication for five articles similar to my idea. Next, I read them and note their style and structure. Finally, I adjust my style to match.

The more you understand your editor, the more you understand her reader. In some cases you may run into lesser editors who "just don't get it." But I've found that most editors have a good grasp of their readers' inner workings and how to serve them best.

If this is 101-level stuff to you, I apologize. I had to say it before moving on to the specifics of how to write engagingly. The key point? All the advice in the next few chapters has to work in service of the editor. Obviously if you're writing for the *New York Times,* you have to use a different style than if you're working for Adobe or Jim's Medical Waste Warehouse.

With that understanding, let's move on to how to write engaging articles.

A Better Mousetrap

Engaging writing doesn't start with engaging writing.

Huh? What?

You could start your articles with sales techniques and tricks to get the reader interested. You could make a lot of empty promises you can't deliver on, and sure, you'll trick the reader into staying with you longer.

Then, in the long run, you'll fall flat on your face.

You can't write engagingly just for the sake of hooking reade and building traffic.

You've got to put your money where your mouth is, or your articles will be like beautifully frosted cakes with sand inside.

So, the first step to engaging writing is to give better advice and better information than everybody else is giving.

This is where our plain ol' journalism tools come in. This isn't a book about journalism, nor would I presume to write one, so I'll do this in a lightning round.

Give Better Advice & Info

To rank, you need to outdo the competition. Nobody needs 500 articles that all say the same thing. If you're writing an informational article, give better information than anybody else. Writing a "How To" article? Give better tips and better actionable advice.

If you're already a subject-matter expert, you won't need to do much research. If you're not, do some digging.

To give better advice and info:

- **Google it.** Do a Google search for each point in your outline you aren't sure about.
- **Reach out to experts.** The ones who've written books (or are selling something) are best. They'll get back to you fast, especially if you offer to promote them with a link.
- **Use good ol' Facebook.** Don't have time to source an expert? Put a shout out on Facebook to see if you know one already.
- **Use Wikipedia.** I know it's demonized, but the site is a gold mine of sources. It's exhaustive, so it's a great place to find things no-one else is saying.

Wikipedia warrants a little more attention. Let's say I'm writing an article called, "Can Dogs Think?"

I search the topic in Wikipedia and find an article with a zillion sources:

(Source: Wikipedia.com)

I won't read them all, but I'll skim the titles, hunting interesting tidbits the other top contenders for my topic aren't giving.

For instance, a Wikipedia source article in a peer-reviewed journal called *Current Biology* found that wolves don't look at human faces. Dogs do, which helps them take cues from their owners and gives a clue to how their minds work. That's not in any of the top Google results for, "can dogs think," but it's a great detail I'll bet my reader will enjoy.

Once you've got all your great advice or information, outline your article. Make each section a single-point lesson that delivers one gold nugget.

I can't overstate the importance of this step. Sure—you understand your reader now. You know his needs and problems. But can you help? And can you help more than those top ten articles in Google are already helping?

If you can't, pack it up. You're trying to sell toothpaste in a world of other people already selling toothpaste.

What Business Strategy Can Teach Us About SEO

In the book, Driven: Business Strategy, Human Actions, and the Creation of Wealth, authors and consultants Joel Litman and Dr. Mark Frigo explain that a unique offering makes all the difference.

"High-performance businesses," they say, "deliver an offering their customers believe is not otherwise available."

Take toothpaste. There's nothing wrong with it as a product. For most of us it's necessary (and for all of us it should be). But it's a commodity. Toothpaste manufacturers like GlaxoSmith-Kline and Colgate-Palmolive are in a cost-plus game. If it costs them $3 to make a tube of toothpaste, you can bet they can only sell it for $3.10 or $3.20. Why? Because if they sell it for $6, their competitors will sell it for $3.10. Nobody will buy the more expensive tube.

That's what Litman and Frigo call "storming a beach head." Everybody else is already there, defending the territory heavily with barbed wire and machine gun emplacements.

That's what we're up against when we write articles that re-hash the same info everybody else is serving up.

Next, look at Microsoft Windows. How much does it cost to produce a copy of that? $3? $2? Less than a tube of toothpaste, probably. Especially when you consider that you hardly ever get a physical disc anymore. But they're not selling copies of MS Windows for $3.10 or $3.20 or $6 even. Sure, it comes prepackaged with many new computers, but it's added to the cost we pay. Buy a copy new via download and it's $139. Why so expensive? Because it's unique. Yes we can use OSX or Linux/Unix, but those are vastly different offerings.

Back when Windows first came out, the price was more like

$450. Bill Gates had created something everybody needed but that nobody could get. As a result, Microsoft wasn't storming a beach head. It was surfing a virgin wave that nobody else was even trying for.

A nice side bonus of building a unique offering like this is value-pricing. The retail price of MS Windows isn't the cost to produce it plus a little more. The price is whatever people will pay, regardless of production cost. It's *whatever it's worth* to people.

That's the kind of thinking we need to take every time we sit down to create a piece of content. We need better information than what everybody else is giving. Use your research skills to double down and get it. Building a unique offering through better information is a step we can't overlook if we want to rank. Better information is a key part of SEO. If we build a unique offering in each piece of content we produce, we'll rank higher, because the searcher will stay on our page a lot longer.

Here's an example of how that works:

Once I had to write an article about cheap beer. I had to rank for the term "cheap beer," but there were already dozens of good articles that listed the ten cheapest brands. Some were written by beer aficionados on sites with high domain authority.

So I did some hard thinking. I don't drink much these days, but I did in college. Back then, was I really concerned with the *cheapest* beer? Or when I asked the question, did I really mean, "the cheapest beer that doesn't taste like cleaning products?"

I did a little skimming through existing articles and noticed nobody was answering that question. So I researched "best tasting beers." I found a few lists of hundreds of beers ranked by drinkability. Then I found some lists of beer brands ranked by price.

I combined the two lists in a Google Sheet and did some fancy sorting. Soon I had a list of the 20 cheapest beers, ranked by drinkability. The coolest part? I embedded the table right at the top of my article so any reader could sort it by cheapest, best-tasting, or by a price/taste multiplier that gave the best of both worlds. (The winner was Narragansett if you're interested.)

Reasoning that my audience was college kids, I added a little college humor to the article, with a sliding flavor scale from "Won't actually make you want to kill yourself" to "You should probably just drink nail polish."

The article hit #1 in Google three days after my editor clicked "publish."

The point? Nobody else had that information. I'd built something unique. Okay, a naked man with a pool toy singing Justin Bieber's "Baby" is unique. But I worked to understand the searcher's unmet need, then built something unique that filled it.

That's SEO.

I'm writing an article right now for Zety.com about JavaScript interview questions. (Still no Pulitzer. I know, I'm shocked.) The other articles online are written by coders. They've all got lists of 20–30 interview questions stuffed with JavaScript coding puzzles.

How can I beat a bunch of coders at that game? I know a little JavaScript, but nobody would call me an expert.

Well, I asked some other coders and tech HR managers to peek at the top three articles for me. I asked if the articles had good info and advice. The answer? Sort of. There's nothing wrong with the JavaScript questions themselves. The problem is in the idea that programming job candidates will face a lot of Java-Script coding questions.

My programming HR experts told me that what really happens is hiring managers in that world are looking for "full stack" developers. That is, people who can do everything from coding to coming up with ideas and solutions to interacting with other employees. They want smart employees, not people who know a certain language back to front. They won't actually ask a lot of JavaScript coding questions in the interview. To paraphrase a whitewater guide instructor who taught me to guide rivers up in Maine decades ago, we can teach a monkey to do JavaScript. What we want is good people.

So—if JavaScript job applicants won't face a lot of coding questions, what will they face instead? General computer science questions, math and logic puzzles, and standard interview questions you'd expect to see in any job interview. Therefore I crafted my article around that idea. Sure my article has coding questions. But it adds the valuable advice to drill those other questions, too. Then it lists dozens of them.

One key point about advice is, make it actionable. Make sure your reader can understand it and do something about it.

At the bottom of this, we're not just writers and content creators. We're detectives. We're building solutions that outdo what's currently available. If we can't do that, we won't rank, and no amount of tricky keyword placement will help us master SEO.

But SEO isn't only about providing better info or advice. Notice too that I put that college humor in my cheap beer article. That was fun, but I didn't do it on a whim. I did it to engage with the reader. To enter into a little conversation with him that he enjoyed. That engagement is the sugar-coating that helps the information go down well. It turns searchers into readers and keeps them on the page instead of clicking back to Google. It's vastly important to SEO, and the next few chapters are all about creating it.

CHAPTER 9:
WRITE ENGAGING
INTRODUCTIONS

Tell me if this sounds familiar:

You do a Google search for something you care about. Maybe your dog is staggering and you're worried sick. You click the first article and start to read.

But the introduction rambles. You can't tell if it'll help. Not wanting to waste time, you click back.

This happens all the time.

That article might give the best info in the world on canine vestibular disease. Why does its unengaging introduction hurt its SEO?

Well, we're human beings, not computers. We're not data-driven. We do things because of how we feel.

Need proof?

In 1997, a neuroscientist named Antonio Damasio made a startling discovery. Studying patients with brain tissue injuries that destroyed their capacity to feel emotion, he found they couldn't make decisions. Given a gambling task, people with emotional impairment couldn't make correct decisions even after they had all the answers.

In other words, emotion doesn't just *influence* decisions. It's at the heart of them.

For more visceral proof we're driven by emotion and not logic, look to the 2016 election. Whatever your political leanings, it's hard to deny that emotion ruled the world on November 8th of that year. Donald Trump is notorious for presenting what Press Secretary Kellyanne Conway called "alternative facts." There's even a webpage dedicated to all the false statements Trump has made, with 240 entries.

So why did Trump win, if not because his facts were more correct than everybody else's? What is he better at than any of the other candidates he ran against?

Creating arousal.

In the book, *Contagious: Why Things Catch On,* viral marketing expert Jonah Berger dedicates 1/6th of the text to emotion and arousal as catalysts to action.

Berger studied thousands of articles from *The New York Times* and *The Wall Street Journal,* focusing on the most-shared posts from those two publications. He found the most-shared articles created arousal. They made people laugh, they made people anxious, they made people angry, or they made people happy.

Those four specific kinds of emotions made people want to share articles with their friends. The more arousal packed into an article, the higher the likelihood it would go viral.

What is Donald Trump if not an arousal-generating tornado? He pumps up those emotions not just in his base, but in his detractors too. Whether his facts are alternative doesn't seem to be the issue. The issue is, he fires people up. He makes his base laugh. He makes them angry at the other side. He plays up their fears and gives them hope that makes them happy. He may not give his enemies a lot of joy, but he certainly stirs up the other emotions in them.

One marketing manager I know even credits Trump with single-handedly reviving Twitter when the social media giants membership was beginning to disintegrate.

According to Berger, it doesn't matter if an emotion is positive or negative as long as it creates arousal. Fear, anger, joy, and humor are arousing. Sadness by contrast is a low-arousal emotion. It therefore discourages readers from sharing articles.

In a perfect example, Berger tells the story of a musician named Dave Carroll. During a 2008 flight on United Airlines, baggage handlers damaged Carroll's $3,500 guitar. After a nine-month runaround, United refused to settle his claim for damages.

Frustrated, Carroll wrote a song about his experience called, *United Breaks Guitars.* The song went viral, getting over 3,000,000 YouTube views within ten days of its release. *Time* magazine ranked it as one of the year's top ten viral videos. United's stock price crashed ten percent four days after Carroll posted the video. That's the equivalent of a $180 million loss.

By now you can guess why Carroll's video went viral. It produced arousal. Lots of it. The incident struck a nerve with millions of frustrated air travelers, tapping into pre-existing anger and getting them to click "share."

But we're not trying to write *viral* articles per se. We're trying to write higher-ranking ones. What does arousal have to do with SEO?

Everything.

Here's why:

1. As we said, Google sees when searchers stay with our pages longer and boosts our rankings.
2. Understanding the searcher through KR, CA, and SMA shows us what the searcher wants.
3. Engaging writing—especially in our introductions— shows the searcher immediately that we understand.

If we can engage emotionally with the searcher fast, we'll inspire action. Namely, the searcher will keep reading.

Doing this sounds tricky, doesn't it? Luckily, we don't have to reinvent the wheel. Lots of smart people have been developing and rigorously testing ways to engage with readers for a long, long time.

What Sales Writing Can Teach Us About SEO

What does sales writing have to do with SEO?

I know, ick. Sales writing. Not the #1 reason anyone got into creating content. Not the #50 reason. And not what anybody wants to read.

So why do I mention it?

Because sales writing has something very much in common with SEO.

It has to hook readers fast.

Sales writing isn't new. It's probably been around for thousands of years. It at least predates the internet. I can remember opening junk mail as a kid when the web was just a gleam in Vint Cerf's eye.

Why is that important? Because it means there's a well-honed art and science to grabbing attention through emotion. It's been tried and tested by millions of writers for at least decades and probably millennia.

In a Copyblogger article, writer Brian Clark shares a piece of writing hailed by many as the most successful sales letter ever.

It was a love letter from *The Wall Street Journal* to prospective customers. It's credited with generating $2 billion in revenue for the paper. Here's how it starts:

Dear Reader:

On a beautiful late spring afternoon, twenty-five years ago, two young men graduated from the same college. They were very much alike, these two young men. Both had been better than average students, both were personable and both – as young college graduates are – were filled with ambitious dreams for the future.

Recently, these two men returned to college for their 25th reunion.

They were still very much alike. Both were happily married. Both had three children. And both, it turned out, had gone to work for the same Midwestern manufacturing company after graduation, and were still there.

But there was a difference. One of the men was manager of a small department of that company. The other was its president.

What Made The Difference

Have you ever wondered, as I have, what makes this kind of difference in people's lives? It isn't always a native intelligence or talent or dedication. It isn't that one person wants success and the other doesn't.

The difference lies in what each person knows and how he or she makes use of that knowledge.

And that is why I am writing to you and to people like you about The Wall Street Journal. For that is the whole purpose of The Journal: To give its readers knowledge – knowledge that they can use in business.

That sales letter uses emotion to hook the reader.

It says, "Here's your heaven and your hell. How do you get one and avoid the other? By reading our paper."

Is that ethical? Well, nobody could argue that the *Wall Street Journal* is bereft of value. If the promise is great business information that provides an edge, it isn't an empty one.

The point? To prove you've got the goods, don't start with a dry, clinical introduction.

Show you understand the reader's pain.

Three Engaging Article Intro Formulas

We need to convince the searcher right away she's in the right place.

To do that, we need to show her:

1. We understand her problem.
2. We feel her pain.
3. We have the solution.

But—

We can't just come out and say that.

If anyone walked up to you on the street and said those things, you'd greet them with 7,000 gallons of suspicion.

So we need to show, not tell. We need to say, "searcher, here's your problem," with fine details. Then we need to say, "here's the emotional pain it's causing you," again, with visceral specifics. Next, we need to say in brief, "here's the solution." Finally, we need to show the emotional effect that solution will have on the reader.

Let's look at three time-tested article intro formulas that show the reader she's in the right place fast.

They're from the world of sales writing and copywriting. They don't fit every kind of writing, but every kind of writing can learn from them. Even if you're writing for *The Smithsonian,* there are gold nuggets here you can use to ramp up reader engagement and SEO.

1. Problem-Agitate-Solution (PAS)

In the Problem-Agitate-Solution intro, we outline the reader's problem, agitate it, and give the solution. It goes like this:

1. Problem. Describe the reader's problem in vivid detail.

2. Agitate. Define the emotions the reader feels because of the problem.
3. Solution. Promise to fix the problem.

Let's say we're writing an article about job searches. This is an easy one for me because I do it all the time.

We've done our research (KR, CA, SMA) so we know the searcher's pain is applying to hundreds of jobs and getting zero reply.

So we start our article like this:

1. Problem:

It's a nightmare. You've applied to hundreds of jobs but you're not getting hired. Worse, nobody is even answering your applications.

2. Agitate:

You're not alone. 200 million people use Indeed to look for jobs each month. That's more than half the US population. With so many job seekers out there, employers are swamped with applications to the point where they can't possibly read all of them. It's no wonder you don't hear back. In fact, it'll be a miracle if you ever get a job at all. You'll be eating Ramen noodles until you're 85.

3. Solution:

Don't panic. Hundreds of thousands of U.S. citizens do get hired each month. There are well-defined ways to boost your chance of being one of them. Read on to see how to use search engines better, why applying via company job sites beats Indeed, and the shocking truth about in-person visits.

I like to add point #4: the feeling the reader will get if she follows my advice:

By the time you close this browser window, you'll have the confidence to step back out into the labor pool, knowing you won't be ignored.

Sound a bit salesy? It is. Again, we won't write every article this way, but we can use elements of the PAS in every article we write.

2. Before-After-Bridge (BAB)

This engaging copywriting introduction formula is similar to the PAS intro I just described. It goes:

1. Before. The reader's world right now.
2. After. What it would feel like to solve the problem.
3. Bridge. How to do it.

Let's say this time we're writing a piece about saving for retirement.

Again, we know the reader's pain and problem, and we've gathered great advice.

1. Before:

Not saving for retirement can lead to waking up at 3am, then staying up. It's no surprise you toss and turn. Fail at saving for retirement and your sunset years could be a long, grim slog.

2. After:

A lucky few have no such worry. They save 10% of their income effortlessly, without noticing they're doing it. They sleep secure in the knowledge they're doing everything they can.

3. Bridge:

What they're doing is called passive saving. They've set up their checking accounts to feed retirement funds automatically every time they cash a paycheck, like a cable payment or a gym subscription. In this article...

Again, this is very similar to the PAS intro. There's nothing magical about it. It just shows we feel the reader's pain and we've got a real solution in our article.

Here's one more:

3. Attention-Interest-Desire-Action (AIDA)

This time-tested copywriting formula is slightly different from the other two. It starts with a hook, sets it deeper, taps into a powerful desire the reader has, and calls for action.

Let's pretend we're writing another job search article. In this one, we'll explain how to get an internship.

1. Attention:

It's the definition of a catch-22. They won't hire you without experience. But you can't get experience without a job.

2. Interest:

Internships to the rescue. Hiring managers are ten times more willing to hire applicants who've held internship positions.

3. Desire:

Internships give you inside information about the job, piles of relevant experience, and networking that can jump-start your career.

4. Action:

The good news? It's not hard to find and get a great internship if you know how. This article is packed with tips to find the best internships, how to land them, and how to use the best internship search websites (including Google!) to get yours fast.

In this case, the *action* we're trying to encourage is reading the rest of the article.

Those are off-the-cuff examples of my three favorite article openings. They're copywriting formulas, so of course you won't follow them slavishly. The important things they have in common are:

1. They show you understand the problem.
2. They show you feel the searcher's pain.

3.   They promise the solution.

In journalism or high-end content marketing, we need to show these things in a different way.

Here's a brilliant, engaging intro from *Forbes*. I found it when I Google-searched "internet of things:"

The "Internet of things" (IoT) is becoming an increasingly growing topic of conversation both in the workplace and outside of it. It's a concept that not only has the potential to impact how we live but also how we work. But what exactly is the "Internet of things" and what impact is it going to have on you, if any? There are a lot of complexities around the "Internet of things" but I want to stick to the basics. Lots of technical and policy-related conversations are being had but many people are still just trying to grasp the foundation of what the heck these conversations are about.

Why is that brilliant? How does it meet our great-introduction-criteria of problem, pain, solution?

Well, the searcher is looking for "internet of things." The writer, Jacob Morgan, presumably did his homework. He got to know the reader's problem, and he felt the reader's pain.

His intro says, in a nutshell:

You searched "internet of things" because you don't know the first thing about it. You don't want a long, drawn-out 10X article that tells you absolutely everything about IoT. You just want the basics. You just want to get in at the ground floor of the discussion. I'm about to show you that.

In other words, it says:

1.   Problem: Everyone is giving you TMI about the IoT.
2.   Emotion: You're frustrated. You don't know "what the heck" it's all about.
3.   Solution: I'm about to give a simple, non-confusing explanation.

Brilliant. Clean. Clear. And no wonder it's the #1 article in Google.

Here's another example. This one is from PetMD. It's the #1 result for "can dogs see color:"

In some ways, humans and dogs see the world very differently. What you perceive as a fire hydrant, your dog sees as a can't-miss communication center. It may look like an ordinary vacuum cleaner to you, but your pooch obviously detects something more sinister lurking in the closet.

One thing we do have in common with our four-legged friends? We see the world in color.

How does this satisfy the problem-emotion-solution need of a great article intro?

It shows the writer grasps the problem—the searcher wants to better understand her dog. Then it feels the searcher's pain. "My poor pooch can't talk. He depends on me to protect him from the scary things in our human world." finally, it serves up the solution. Surprisingly, dogs *do see in color.*

And (by inference) read on to learn more from these obviously knowledgeable experts.

That's a great intro. One more way it connects with the reader is with a cool video right above the text. Interspersed with shots of slow-motion dogs making cute facial expressions into the camera, animal experts talk. We can't hear them unless we turn the sound on, but we can see from onscreen text they're talking about color vision in dogs.

In short, we know with 100% certainty that we've come to the right place.

We can see at a glance that not only does this article know what we're asking, but it knows *why we're asking it* (our emotions). Finally, it has the right solution to our question.

This doesn't always have to be an overt process. In an article called *Taste the Season at Sushi Sora* by travel and food writer Chris Dwyer, the introduction unfurled like this:

"The extraordinary spread of metropolitan Tokyo, all the way to the magical silhouette of Mount Fuji on the horizon, has few better vantage points than from Mandarin Oriental, Tokyo. From every room, the cityscape unfurls beneath you, while from the sushi counter at Sushi Sora, the vast floor-to-ceiling window offers uninterrupted views toward the Tokyo Skytree and far beyond."

Where's the problem, emotion, and solution there?

Well, Dwyer understands his reader very well. He knows she's in love with exotic locales and breathtaking views. She wants a new experience. He taps into how that would feel for her, and promises to deliver it.

We need to communicate to the searcher as fast as possible that 1) I understand your question, 2) I feel the arousal that made you type it into Google (fear, pain, anger, excitement, hope, desire), and 3) I have the answer you are looking for.

If you can communicate all that in a few sentences, the reader is hooked.

The most important part of this? Prove you've actually got the searcher's answer.

Let's look at introductions from the top two articles in Google for "dog staggering:"

From WagWalking.com:

Should your dog be staggering, he may appear as if he is drunk. You may observe him appearing uncoordinated, having difficulty walking straight, and falling down on occasion. Staggering is often the result of vestibular disease, which impacts the balance systems of your dog's body. The disease is the result of irritation to the nerves that connect the inner ear to the brain. When this occurs, it leads to a loss of balance along with other issues.

Not exactly Hamlet, but it does the job. Here's why it works:

1. It tells the reader, "Here's your problem. Your dog is staggering and even falling down." The reader says, "Yes, you're right. That's my exact problem."
2. It tells the reader why it happens. The reader thinks, "Okay, this writer knows what's going on."
3. It promises more info. The reader sees, *"along with other issues"* and thinks, "I'd better keep reading."

The emotion step is gone. The intro works anyway (and the article ranks #1 in Google) because the reader is worried. The emotionless style feels somewhat like a conversation with a calming, knowledgeable doctor.

Here's another good introduction:

From WebMD:

Little kids love spinning in place until they fall down. But when we're talking about our dogs, there's really no good reason for loss of balance.

So why do dogs fall down? Is it possible to treat loss of balance? And when should your canine companion see a vet?

That's clean and quick. Right away we get an emotional nudge comparing dizzy dogs to spinning kids. Then we get three promises:

We'll learn why dogs fall down, if we can fix it, and when we should take Penny to the vet.

I assume the writer did her research, so she knows the reader is most interested in finding answers to those questions in particular.

Both intros:

1. Show the writer understands the reader's problem.
2. Say the solution is in the article.

Do we always need so much emotion?

That depends on your searcher. You've done the research, so you know her intimately. If she's a programmer, the touchy-feely stuff might turn her off.

If you Google-search the different Object Oriented Programming (OOP) concepts, you'll find a lot of articles by a guy named Thorben Janssen. Thorben writes perfect introductions for his audience (and perfect articles). That's why he ranks. But he doesn't talk about the reader's night sweats in his intros. He just lays it plain. Here's one of his article introductions:

The word polymorphism is used in various contexts and describes situations in which something occurs in several different forms. In computer science, it describes the concept that objects of different types can be accessed through the same interface. Each type can provide its own, independent implementation of this interface. It is one of the core concepts of object-oriented programming (OOP).

If you're wondering if an object is polymorphic, you can perform a simple test. If the object successfully passes multiple is-a or instanceof tests, it's polymorphic. As I've described in my post about inheritance, all Java classes extend the class Object. Due to this, all objects in Java are polymorphic because they pass at least two instanceof checks.

About as emotional as a steel ingot. But loud and clear he says, "I know why you Googled "what is polymorphism" and I know exactly how to answer you."

In journalism, one popular introduction style is to "set the hook" with a story about a strong protagonist.

In the April 2018 issue of *Discover,* writer Sarah Scoles wrote her introduction this way:

"Astrophysicist Jean-Peirre Luminet didn't have a supercomputer when he showed the world what a black hole looks like. He just had an IBM 7040 and a bunch of punch cards. He knew from theory that black holes do not emit light. But the material that swirls around them—dust and gas stripped from stars—shines all the way to its

inanimate death. Light from that material, Luminet thought, would trace the black hole's shape, including warps in space-time from its extreme gravity."

That's gripping and emotional. It's from a print magazine, but I'd argue that online it'd make pretty solid SEO. Why? Because the reader would stick with it.

In the book *On Writing Well,* author William Zissner says, "The most important sentence in any article is the first one. If it doesn't induce the reader to proceed to the second sentence, your article is dead."

There are a million ways to do this right. It's more art than science. But at the core, make sure you don't confuse the searcher. Don't make her think. Don't make her wonder, "Am I in the right place?" Roll out the welcome mat by showing you know why she searched and that you have the answer.

Engaging Section Introductions

Before we move on to Chapter 10: Soothe Your Reader's Pain by Cutting Out the Fat, we need to cover one more point about engaging introductions.

Introductions aren't only for the beginning of our article. They're for the start of every section too.

The idea is like this:

If your article solves a problem for the searcher, then the sections of your article solve parts of that problem.

The article intro proves you understand the problem and the feeling that goes with it, and it says you'll give the solution in the article.

Every section intro has to do that in miniature.

Your article introductions might be 100–200 words long. Your section introductions only need to be about 30–50. But just like your article intro, each section intro needs to telegraph the problem you'll solve and the emotion that goes with it.

Now if you use the PAS intro formula to write the introductions to all your articles and all your sections, your content will be a little bit like sneakers in a dryer.

To avoid that, I like to take a little head-scratching time to pace around the house and think, "What slice of the major problem does this section solve?"

Then I like to vary back and forth between pleasure and pain. Heaven and hell.

Let's revisit our internship article example.

When I actually wrote that article, I used an AIDA intro:

In 7 minutes, you'll know how to get an internship like you were born to it. But first—

Meet the hiring manager, Luanne.

She's guarding your dream job.

Nice transparent glasses frames.

She's ten times more likely to hire you if you've held internship positions.

Internships give you inside job knowledge, valuable, relevant experience, and networking worth its weight in gold.

Finding internships is about the most important thing a college grad can do.

The good news is, it's easy once you know the steps.

That's a solid AIDA intro. It shows I understand the searcher's problem and emotions, and it promises a good solution.

One of the sections in the article was, "How to Find Internships Fast With Job Fairs and Networking."

I kicked it off with pleasure/heaven:

Imagine it's five months from now.

You not only figured out how to find an internship—

You also got your dream job.

Maybe you found it on the internship websites.

But—it's even money you got it networking or at a job fair.

Okay, so a little heavy on the em-dash, but you get the point. I'm saying, "Hey reader, here's what you really want, and I'm about to tell you how to get it."

The next section starts with pain/hell. It's about how to make your own internships:

Networking, job fairs, internship websites...

They're popular ways to get an internship. Maybe too popular.

What do I mean?

You'll battle hundreds of others for the same positions.

So, don't rely on internship finders alone. Find internships nobody's trying for because they don't exist.

See that? It starts out with pain and fear.

The point? You don't always have to use the same emotion in every article intro or section intro. Use your KR, CA, and SMA research to understand the searcher's needs and feelings. Then pick different emotions to tap into on a case-by-case basis, tying each choice into the problem you're promising to solve.

This is SEO. It's not image alt attributes. It's not metadata. I'll cover those things at the end of the book if you're interested or because clients are demanding them. But one of the most central factors in good SEO is the ability to connect with the reader right away. Write engaging introductions and you're halfway there. Get the searcher to stay with you longer than she stays with anybody else, and Google will notice you. In result, your articles will dominate the rankings.

But what about the part of your article after the introduction? That's up next.

CHAPTER 10: SOOTHE YOUR READER'S PAIN BY CUTTING OUT THE FAT

Engaging writing is the only way to show your reader you can help.

Do it right, and she's hooked. She'll stay with you and Google will grant higher rankings and more traffic.

Do it wrong, and even if you understand her better than any other writer, she won't know. She'll click back to Google, and you'll sink.

By now, you know you need engaging introductions. But writing an engaging 100–200 words is not enough.

At an ASJA conference, I met an editor from a massive online publication. I really wanted to write for her. Someone introduced us and I asked if I could pitch some stories.

"I'm up to my eyeballs in pitches," she said. "What I really need is writers who can write engagingly. I have three right now. I need 30."

Well, that's what every editor needs most. Even if you take the extra time to read the searcher's mind and heart, and even if you prove you've done that in the introduction, you can lose her if you don't keep up the two-way conversation.

The good news? It's not hard to write engagingly. Anyone can learn it. We're not trying to win Pulitzers with SEO work. If our goal is to show the reader we understand her plight, it's easy.

The first way is to keep it brief.

On Writing Well

Over 30 years ago, New York journalist and teacher William Zinsser delivered a lecture to his students that went over well. He turned that lecture into a popular audio recording and later a book called *On Writing Well*. The message is simple: Don't overdo it.

Over and over again throughout his book, Zinsser exhorts writers to cut the fat. To take out adverbs. (Or, as Stephen King says, "The adverb is not your friend.") To use short sentences. To use short words with Germanic roots instead of long, latinate ones. (Think "give up" instead of "relinquish," "ask" instead of "inquire," and "flag" not "indicator." There's a great Wikipedia list that pits long words against their short cousins.) "Clear thinking," Zinsser says, "becomes clear writing. One can't exist without the other."

Zinsser also counsels us to avoid jargon and keep it personal. "Writing," he says, "is an intimate transaction between two people, conducted on paper, and it will go well to the extent that it retains its humanity."

Zinsser asks us to get out of the reader's way by cutting everything we can. Never use two words where one will do.

Author James Kilpatrick describes Zinsser's central thesis as, "Writing improves in direct ratio to the number of things we can keep out of it."

Zinsser called clutter "the disease of American writing." He said we're "strangling in unnecessary words."

"The secret of good writing," he says, "is to strip every sentence to its cleanest components."

Does this sound like a dumbing down? Zinsser doesn't think so. If the reader is lost, he says, it's because the writer wasn't careful enough. It's not because the reader isn't smart enough to understand our ornate language.

He asks us to say, "now" instead of "at this point in time," and, "it's raining" instead of, "at the present time we are experiencing precipitation."

How does Zinsser's advice connect to SEO?

Well, remember my story about being at the boat launch with the barking dogs and screaming kids? My outboard motor was flooded. I grabbed my phone and typed in, "outboard motor won't start."

The last thing I wanted was to read a long, well-written diatribe on outboard motors. I wanted plain English and as few words as possible. I wanted my motor to start. I found all kinds of long analyses of why two-stroke engines fail to start. The most helpful piece of content though just said, "You've probably flooded it. If so, you can try a hot start. That's where you crank the throttle all the way open, wait a minute, and turn the key."

There was a short explanation of why the trick would work that sounded plausible. I tried it and vroom! The engine roared to life and we were off to splash and play.

Fight Clutter

If clutter is like weeds, how do we fight it? One editor I worked for gave me a valuable tool. The first time my writing students heard it, they weren't impressed. But I kept after them until they started using it. After they tried it a few times, they came to see it as one of the most valuable SEO tools in their inventory.

This is what the editor told me that was so valuable:

"You're good, but your work is sloppy. You need to proofread. I know—after you've worked on a piece for hours and your eyes hurt and it's finished, you just want to turn it in and never look at it again. But that's exactly when taking one more read-through of it is the most valuable thing you can do."

Shout out to Frank Moraes from HTML.com. I've used that trick for years to wow editors and keep searchers on the page ever since.

Zinsser recommends reading your piece aloud, but I'll go him one better because I was born later and I have the benefit of tech. Have Siri or Google Assistant read it to you. I do it while I'm out for a run or eating lunch. You'll be stunned how many extra words, flubs, and awkward constructions stand out like someone splashed them in neon paint.

Here's a screenshot from the version history of Chapter 4:

sprinklers will probably show up about 30 times naturally anyway. If it shows up 90 times, you're either stuffing keywords in on purpose or you have a small vocabulary.

When I'm done writing a piece, I go back to my keyword research spreadsheet and look at it again. I look check to see if my focus keyword is spread throughout my piece about 1% of the time. I check to see if the other terms in my spreadsheet show up here and there. If they don't, maybe it means I've missed a point I should've covered—for the reader's sake.

But I never try to stuff more keywords in for Google's sake.

The bottom line? Use Yoast to keep yourself from going overboard and making Google angry. But always come back to the reader's needs. Keep those as true North, and you won't go wrong.

Pulling it All Together

Should you try to write an article that bundles in all the terms and topics in your keyword research?

Probably not. Unless you're writing a 10x article called *The Ultimate Guide to Real Estate Investing for Beginners*, you shouldn't slavishly dump all these phrases into it.

But if you're targeting "real estate investing" pay attention to them. You should at least realize, because your reader is preoccupied with cares about them. If those sentence

The more you get out of the reader's way, the faster your great info gets into her head. She'll appreciate it and stick with you, and Google will notice.

Cut the extra, ~~cut the extra, cut the extra. I can't say it enough~~.

Use the HemingwayApp to Keep it Brief

Having a hard time keeping it short?

Try the HemingwayApp.

Many thanks to Natalie Severt of Zety (formerly Uptowork) for turning me on to this one. It's an app that analyzes your content for brevity. When I first used it, I found it annoying, but now I see the value in it. I try to take its suggestions whenever possible. It's free to use the online version, or you can buy the download version, which they've made more convenient in the name of revenue.

The app identifies long, confusing sentences (in yellow), *very* long, confusing sentences (in red) and adverbs (in blue). It also calls out uses of the passive voice and long, latinate words.

for her. Someone introduced us and I asked if I could pitch some stories.

"I'm up to my eyeballs in pitches," she said. "What I really need is writers who can write engagingly. I have three right now. I need 30."

Well, that's what every editor needs most. Even if you take the extra time to read the searcher's mind and heart, and even if you prove you've done that in the introduction, you can lose her if you don't keep up the two-way conversation.

The good news? It's not hard to write engagingly. Anyone can learn it. We're not trying to win Pulitzers with SEO work. If our goal is to show the reader we understand her plight, it's easy.

The first way is to keep it brief.

On Writing Well

Over 30 years ago, New York journalist and teacher William Zinsser delivered a lecture to his students that went over well. He turned that lecture into a popular audio recording and later a book called *On Writing Well*. The message is simple: Don't overdo it.

Hemingway *Editor*

Readability

Grade 4
Good

Words: **1125**
Show More ▾

8 adverbs, meeting the goal of 13 or fewer.

4 uses of passive voice, meeting the goal of 19 or fewer.

1 phrase has a simpler alternative.

8 of 95 sentences are hard to read.

1 of 95 sentences is very hard to read.

When I write an article for the web, I run it through the app and break up long sentences. I usually score pretty well on the other metrics from the start, but I peek at my numbers just in case.

Check Your Work With Yoast

If you write with WordPress, you've got another tool to keep your writing short and readable: the Flesch Reading Ease test. The test checks your sentence length and word length like the Hemingway App, then gives you a percent score.

Yoast also checks your section length, word-repetition, and other gewgaws.

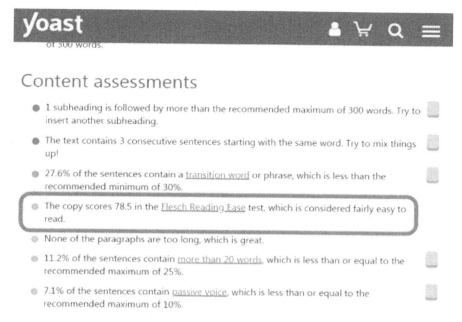

Does this all matter for SEO? Does Google care if our sentences and words are short? It may. In a way it would make sense if Google's algorithm used something like the Hemingway App to check our content. But in another way it wouldn't, because then it would select against "richer" publications like *The New York Times* or *The Atlantic.* Some searchers don't *want* short sentences and short words, so why punish them?

But think about this: if you cut a lot of extra words from your content, then you are in a way, making literary maple syrup. You are cutting out a lot of things that are not keywords. That alone should make Google's algorithm like your content more. But there's another, beefier reason to cut out extra words.

If short sentences, short paragraphs, and shorter words matter to SEO (and I firmly believe they do) I think it's mainly because the searcher is in a hurry. She sat down and Google-searched because she wanted to know something. Most of the time, that doesn't mean she wants to read an epic.

So, it's not so much that Google's algorithm likes tersely–worded text. It's more that the reader likes it and Google sees what the reader likes.

A Word About Engaging Writing

Beyond just cutting out the extra, how can we "write engagingly?"

We're already doing part of it by doing our research. CR, CA, and SMA get us to understand our searcher's needs and feelings. That means when we write, we can personalize *the way* we say it to that reader.

Some writers swear by creating a vivid image of the reader in their minds before they start to write. I like to do this because it makes the writing feel like a one-on-one conversation with a friend. Since I started doing it, I get lots of emails from readers telling me they feel like we had a two-way conversation.

Another way to write engagingly is to look at what's already working well, then imitate it. Go back to your Ahrefs account or SEMRush or Grepwords. Type the URL of the site you're writing for and hit [Enter]. The articles that pop up first are its highest-traffic articles. Read them. What about their style do you think connects so well with readers?

(Source: SEMRush.com)

I can't click through to the articles without a paid subscription, but I can see their URLs and find them easily enough by Googling "engadget" + "youtube" and so on.

Then, if I'm writing for engadget, I can get a sense of the engaging style of its top-performing posts.

Every site or blog will have its own way to engage with the reader. In general, keep it brief, give better info, and stay connected to your reader's feelings.

A lot of that comes down to how you structure content. We'll get to that in a bit, but first a word about ramping up the value in your content.

CHAPTER 11: BUILD EMPATHY WITH BETTER STRUCTURE

I have bad news.

Your reader? Alice?

She's a skimmer.

She didn't come to read your finely crafted wordsmithing. She's not looking to be awed by your clever use of metaphor and simile. She's trying to accomplish a task. In her ideal world, she'll ask a question and you'll answer in five seconds. Maybe she'll like the answer so much she'll stick around to learn more.

But she doesn't want that when she Googles something. She just wants the answer so she can get on with her day.

But—

If you give the answer in three seconds, won't your rankings suffer?

Well if she clicks back to Google, you're in trouble. Google thinks you didn't help her. But if she closes the browser window, satisfied, and does not return to Google, you're okay. In that case, Google knows she got what she was after.

But you want her to stay on your page anyway.

You're not looking to answer her question in three seconds

and hear, "Thanks, bye."

You want her to view or click your ads. You want her to sign up for your SaaS or buy your product.

So, you need her to stay.

That's the struggle.

According to Nielsen, web users mostly skim content, spending 80% of their time on an article's introduction. They read only 20% of the text on a page. Coschedule adds that only 1 in 5 web users actually reads an entire post.

That's like if you wrote a book and only 1/5th of the people who bought it actually read it, while the rest just read the chapter headings, then returned it for a refund.

Check out the eye-tracking heat map below (used under Wikimedia Commons license). It shows where searchers looked on a web page.

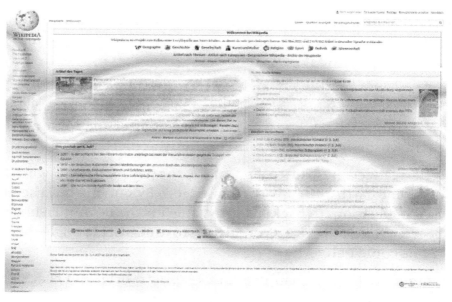

Visitors to this page focus mostly on the introduction and images. Users tend to focus mostly on introductions (80.3%), the left side of the page, headings, and images.

So—if Alice mainly reads our introduction, then glances at headings and images before jumping ship, how can we get her to stick around longer?

Answer:

With better introductions, headings, and images. In a nutshell, with better structure.

Less Words

Wait—write *less* words in our articles? What about 10X content? What about writing bigger, longer, better articles? What about being comprehensive and giving the reader 10 times more value than any other article?

Better doesn't mean longer. More value doesn't mean more words.

Remember my pontoon boat story? The reader is in a hurry. She's busy working on work, on home and family chores, or on having fun with friends. Most of us don't *want* to spend more time with our phone, tablet, or computer. We just want *the answer*, and we want it now.

One of my writing students ran into a problem with this. As he cut the fat out of his articles, he found he didn't have much left. He'd start with a 1,200-word article, but after chopping all the extra words, his articles were coming in at half the size.

He realized he had to find more content. More answers to different parts of the reader's question. By cutting out the fat, he'd made room to pack in more value for the reader. To find it, he went back to his KR, CA, and SMA to dig up other angles benefits he could deliver.

I talked a lot last chapter about keeping it brief. But that's not just to stay engaging. It's to give the reader what she wants in an eyeblink.

How can we do that and still keep the reader on the page?

By adding more value and using the inverted pyramid.

Inverted Pyramid

Most journalists and content creators have heard of this.

Here it is in a nutshell (from Wikimedia Commons)—

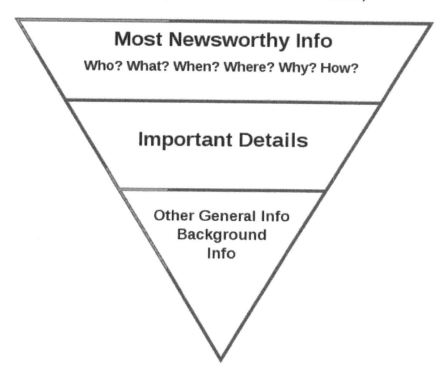

The gist?

Put the most important stuff up top. Structure it so what your searcher cares about most is right in her face when she clicks through from Google.

You *know* what's most important to her because you did your research (KR, CA, SMA).

Now show her at a glance you've structured things this way.

The next step? Writing better headlines.

Write Better Headlines

If you want the reader to know you "get her," what's the most bang for your buck?

You already know the answer, because I put it in the headline of this section.

The single most important way to engage with your reader is to write great headlines.

Engaging, descriptive headlines tell your reader you know the reason for her search. They show you feel her pain and you've got the answers she wants most.

Great headlines turn skimmers into readers.

Let's break great headlines down into article headlines and section headings.

Write Better Article Headlines (H1s)

The article headline (H1) is the most important part of your content.

In HTML-speak, the title of an article is called the H1. A section heading is an H2, and ever-smaller headings are H3s, H4s, H5s, and H6's respectively.

If your headline doesn't show the reader you know why she searched (and that you can deliver) she won't click it.

I'm not talking about clickbait.

Ranker compiled a list of the worst clickbaity headlines. Here are some:

- This Girl Didn't Know What's Inside Her, Not Until They Cut Off Her Pants! Shocking!
- Man creates brain-dead simple system to cutting your grocery bill by 90% (HINT: It's NOT Coupons)
- When You Read These 19 Shocking Food Facts, You'll

Never Want To Eat Again
- This Intense Footage Will Shake Even The Most Skeptic Non-Believer
- This Is Not A Joke. You May Laugh, But You Shouldn't. It's Quite Horrifying.

Those headlines may make us want to click, but they're not good SEO.

They're clickbait. The sites that publish them don't expect to rank in Google.

How can I tell?

They don't have keywords. They don't tell me what the articles are about. They promise I'll be shocked, stunned, disgusted, shaken, and amused, but nothing more.

Only two hint at a topic. One is "food facts" and the other is "grocery bill." But if I Google-search the topics, neither headline ranks.

For "save on groceries," here's what does:

1. 15 Ways to Save Money on Groceries
2. Lesson 1: How to Save $100 or More at Grocery Stores
3. 30 Clever Ways to Save Money on Groceries
4. How to Save Money on Groceries
5. How to Save Money on Groceries
6. How to Save Money on Groceries (And Eat Like Royalty)
7. 25 Budget Grocery Shopping Tips to Save Money
8. 84 Insanely Easy Ways to Save Money on Groceries
9. 20 Simple Ways to Save Money On Groceries
10. How to Save Money on Groceries - Top 20 Ways to Save

Almost all those headlines assume one thing: if I search, "how to save on groceries" I want to know how to save money on groceries. (Safe bet, right?)

Those headlines parrot back what the searcher asked. They put the keywords right in the headline. They don't do it to trick Google's algorithm. They do it to connect with the searcher. Just like if you open a grocery store, you don't want people to think of you as a yarn store that also sells stationery and food-stuffs.

But if the headlines are all pretty much the same, why does article #1 rank higher than the rest? If I had to guess, I'd say it gives the best info in the most concise way. It satisfies more readers.

The #2 article takes a different slant (which I think is why it outranks the others). It says, "Hey, you can find ways to save money on groceries in these other articles. Want to learn how to save $100? Click here."

I clicked and guess what? It has the same info as the other posts. I'm convinced it ranks #2 because it promised something different, then didn't totally disappoint. (But as the searcher, I would have been happier if it showed me how to save $100, even if it was spread out over a month.)

So, putting your focus keyword in your H1 is rule #1. But you do want to make it clickable (NOT clickbait.)

Must you always write generic headlines if you want to rank? No. A headline like, "MIT Researchers Find Way to Save $1,000 a Year on Groceries" can rank high because it's different. Content creators often take the easy path because it works.

Write Clickable Headlines

You don't have to use formulas to have great SEO. In fact, it's better if you understand *why* the headline formulas below work, then use your creativity to see what else you can come up with.

Think of the ideas below like training wheels. But of course feel free to use them. They dominate the top results in Google with good reason.

- XYZ Guide (Software Engineer Resume Guide)
- 10 [Easy, Simple, Fast, Quick, Proven] Ways to XYZ (10 Proven Ways to Save More of Every Paycheck)
- How to XYZ (How to Stay Asleep Longer)
- Ultimate Guide to XYZ (Ultimate Guide to Investing)
- X# Reasons You're [XYZ undesired outcome] (25 Reasons Your Hair is Falling Out)
- Here's a [Technique, Trick, Method] That's Helping XYZ to XYZ (Here's a Technique That's Helping Children Learn Math Faster)
- X# Tips from Experts About How to XYZ (30 Tips from Experts for How to Get a Green Job Fast)
- Here's a Fast Way to [solve XYZ problem] (Here's a Fast Way to Stop Drinking Coffee Now)
- X# Secrets to XYZ (27 Secrets to Save on Heating Bills)
- What XYZ Says About XYZ (What Industry Insiders Say About Learning Scrum)
- Stop XYZ [problem] Once and for All (Stop Overeating Once and for All)
- X# Hacks to [XYZ] (20 Hacks to Organize Your Garage in a Day)
- Now You Can [do XYZ you want][while also doing XYZ] (Now You Can Start a $2,000 a Month Business While Working Your Day Job)
- [Do XYZ] Like XYZ (Clean Your Teeth Like a Dentist)
- Build an [XYZ, or "Have an" XYZ] You Can Be Proud Of (Have Cooking Skills You Can Be Proud Of)

There are dozens more possibilities for H1s. One of my favorite digital marketing writers, Sarah Peterson, wrote a great article for Sumo with 51 of them.

Do those headline ideas seem salesy? They are. But you don't need to write your headlines like that.

Remember your editor and publication. Your headlines should fit the outlet. But they should contain the key elements of the salesy H1 formulas above.

Each H1 you write must convince the searcher you:

1. Know the problem.
2. Understand the feeling it creates.
3. Solve it in your article.

There's even an online tool called the Coschedule Headline Analyzer that will score your headlines for you. It's a fun and useful tool as long as you don't blindly accept its judgements as SEO gospel.

What about section headings?

That's next.

Write Better Section Headings (H2s)

Your article headings (H1s) get searchers to click. Do them right, and your searcher is now a skimmer.

But your section headings turn those skimmers into readers.

Each section heading (H2) needs to work like a mini-article-headline. It needs to make the skimmer stop and say, *"Whoa. I need to read this section."* (Remember the goal: keep the searcher on the page longer.)

In an article from the National Institutes of Health (NIH) about talking to kids about marijuana, the H2s are:

1. Why do young people use marijuana?
2. How can I prevent my child from using marijuana?
3. Marijuana can be addictive.
4. Marijuana is unsafe if you're behind the wheel.
5. Marijuana is linked to school failure, lower income, and poorer quality of life.
6. Marijuana is linked to some mental illness.

You can bet people who search this topic don't want their kids smoking, but they know they can't just say, "Because it's wrong." Their kids are telling them it's safer than alcohol. This article gives them something to grab onto. It gives them ammo in an argument. (I'm not judging the ethics of that. I'm only saying the article ranks high in Google because it gives the searcher what she wants.)

Make your H2s work like mini-headlines like that. How? Put important keywords in them. Put the most important keywords near the top. Those are the ones from your research with the most monthly search traffic.

Put the least important toward the bottom.

If you structure your outline that way, when Alice skims your work, she'll say, "Wow. This piece has everything I'm wondering about."

Then she'll stop skimming and start reading.

This is *not* a trick to outsmart Google. It's to show your reader that your article has what she wants. That's a fine distinction, but important.

Here's an example of how this works.

I had to write an article that ranked for "jobs for the disabled" and related keywords.

My article's H1 was "100+ Great Jobs for People with Disabilities to Get You Out and Earning."

That H1 has the highest-traffic keyword from my KR ("jobs for people with disabilities").

It also understands the searcher's problem and emotion (it's harder to find a job when you're disabled, and it's frustrating to be cooped up and dependent on others for money.)

I wrote these section headings/H2s:

1. Jobs for Physically Disabled People
2. Jobs for People with ADD/ADHD
3. Jobs for Individuals With Mental Illness

4. Jobs for People With Learning Disabilities
5. Government Jobs for Disabled Individuals
6. Jobs for People With Intellectual Disabilities
7. Jobs for Deaf and Hearing Impaired People
8. Careers for the Blind and Visually Impaired
9. Jobs for Disabled People With Speech Impairments
10. Jobs for People With Anxiety Disorder Disabilities
11. Disability Jobsites

Each of those terms came straight from my keyword research. The first had the most monthly traffic. The #11 H2 (disability jobsites) had the least. The article grabbed Google's coveted featured snippet.

If we Google "talk to kids about drugs," the first article that pops up has this H1: "Talking to Your Child About Drugs (for Parents).

It has these H2s:

1. Preschool to Age 7
2. Ages 8 to 12
3. Ages 13 to 17
4. Laying Good Groundwork

You can bet that article nailed the search intent better than the others. It realized (probably through KR, CA, and SMA) that the searcher's most pressing question is how to talk to kids by age.

Use Skim Stoppers

There's more to stopping skimmers than eye-catching H2s.

Put other "skim-stoppers" in your toolbox, too.

The go-to favorites are bullet lists, tables, bold font, and attention-grabbing phrases.

Bullet Lists and Tables

Use bullet lists and tables to stop skimmers in their tracks.

Heat map studies show even if readers ignore other content, they stick to bullet lists like junkyard magnets.

But—

Don't slap just any bullet list into your article.

Build bullet lists around keywords. When the searcher stops to read the list, the words in it will catch her eye.

That'll turn her from a skimmer to a reader.

Here's an example from real life:

Let's say you've got Lyme disease and you're fed up with waking up at 3am. Lying frustrated in bed, you search, "Lyme disease sleep."

The first thing that pops up is an article on TreatLyme.net called *Sleep in Lyme Disease: The Basic Steps.*

First, it's the perfect headline. It shows the writer grasps the reader's problem and is offering solutions.

Next, it's got good H2s:

1. The Problem with Sleep in Lyme Disease
2. Problems that Cause Poor Sleep in Lyme Disease Treatment
3. First, Lower Cytokines for Sleep in Lyme Disease
4. Second: Use Good Hygiene for Sleep in Lyme Disease
5. Third: Correct Underlying Medical Problems for Sleep in Lyme Disease
6. Finally: Use Supplements for Medications for Sleep in Lyme Disease

Those H2s show at a glance that this article is packed with unique, helpful information. It's not just advice to try melatonin or cut screen time like everybody else is giving.

They're also a little ham-fisted in their use of keywords. The writer didn't need to hammer "Sleep in Lyme Disease" in every heading. He obviously did it for Google's benefit. Never a good idea. The article ranks high in spite of trying that bald-faced trick.

Better to put *variations* of the main keywords into each H2. I probably would have put some combination of, "Lyme," "Disease," and "Sleep" in every one.

That aside, the article uses bullet lists as skimmer-stopping roadblocks.

Here's its Hemingwayesque introduction:

Most people have problems with getting enough restorative sleep in Lyme disease. Lack of adequate sleep

- *worsens pain,*
- *causes fatigue,*
- *increases inflammation cytokines, and*
- *suppresses the immune system.*

A restorative amount of sleep is seven to nine hours to correct these problems.

As a chronic Lyme sufferer, that hits me where I live. Does it seem unemotional? It's not. It presses all the buttons on my worst fears around Lyme-induced insomnia. But it does it fast, with a bullet list I can read even laying down in the pitch black with the screen brightness set to minimum.

The next section tells *why* Lyme robs sleep. Again it includes a skim-stopping bullet list:

- *excess inflammation cytokines produced by the immune system,*
- *poor sleep hygiene,*
- *hormone dysfunction,*
- *sleep apnea,*
- *night time urination,*
- *restless legs syndrome,*

- *anxiety about sleep,*
- *depression,*
- *pain,*
- *herbal and prescription medication side effects, and*
- *the use of alcohol and/or caffeine.*

Those are all things I care about, so I stop skimming to read the section carefully. The list is packed with LSI keywords like, "sleep apnea" and "anxiety about sleep."

Are bullet lists great journalism? That's for others to decide. If we want great SEO—and we know the key is to engage the reader—then lists and tables are a useful tool.

Use Bold to Catch the Reader's Eye

Another great way to get a skimmer reading is with boldface font.

But use it sparingly.

I like to use bold with short, eye-catching phrases about once per section. Sometimes I'll put keywords in them. In an article about how to start a cover letter, I might say...

Every cover letter needs a hook.

...then explain why.

Mostly though, I used bold to highlight what I call "heads-up" phrases. They're imperatives we use all the time in everyday speech to get listeners to focus on our words.

Here are a few example heads-up phrases:

- Heads up!
- Consider this:
- The secret?
- This is vital:
- Here's a nightmare:
- Warning!

- Wait, what?
- But beware.
- Congrats!
- Be careful.
- Excuse me?
- Important:
- Catastrophe.
- Success!
- Here's a secret:
- Hey, wait!
- Most people don't know this:
- Oh-oh.
- Ready, set—
- But—
- Guess what?

There are dozens of variations. As with most SEO writing, it can be a little salesy and it doesn't work in every publication. But even if your skim stoppers are less like a call-to-action from a 1990s, generally you can find one phrase per section to put in bold.

Link Out to Good Sources

Do you "link out?" You should. But there's a right way and a wrong way.

For years people thought they shouldn't link to external sources. The fear is that when we put links in our pages, we pass PageRank on to other articles.

PageRank is a term created by Google founders Sergey Brin and Larry Page. It assigns a score to each web page on a scale of 1–10 based on relevance and authority. Some online tools purport to tell you a site's PageRank, but Google doesn't reveal that data, so those tools are estimating.

The fears about linking out are half right.

We don't want to link out to "the competition." That's any page that already ranks high for the focus keyword you're targeting.

So—if you're trying to rank for "cheap Hatchimals," you shouldn't link to another page that already ranks for that.

Why not?

Because if you do, you're telling Google, "This other page you already like is the source I used. It's the authority on the topic. I'm not saying anything new. My article is redundant and you can ignore it."

Google will nod and give that existing page a little more esteem. In the process it'll give you a little less.

However, Google almost certainly likes it when we link out to reputable sources in a way that helps the reader. That's according to Rand Fishkin and just about every other SEO guru out there.

Let's say you're writing a piece about how to save money for college. You do your research and write a great article with attention-getting headings, bullet lists, and other skim-stoppers.

But in one case, you don't link out to any sources. In another, you link to valuable resources that help your reader:

- FinAid.org's Student Budget Calculator
- Mint.com for tracking finances
- Scholarships.com for slashing college bills

Most SEO pros think Google's algorithm probably rewards that. Even better, those links are useful to your reader. You're providing resources that meet her needs.

Again, she'll see the links and stop skimming to see what they're about. (Especially if they have keyword in them that she recognizes.) That means she'll stay with you longer. And that— again—means Google will reward you.

Through trial, error, and research, I've come to believe certain links are better than others when it comes to linking out:

- .org domains
- .edu domains
- .gov domains
- Scientific publications found on Google Scholar
- Any page with a high Page Authority (PA) or Domain Authority (DA)

Why are those links better SEO? Google respects them.

Break Up Long Paragraphs

Are we engaged in dumbing down our content?

Maybe.

Or maybe it's just hard to read on screens.

Either way, shorter paragraphs turn skimmers into readers.

According to Yoast, big walls of text scare readers. They're hard to skim. Readers see them and think, "This might answer my question or it might not. There's no way to tell without reading the whole thing. I don't have time I'll click back to Google and see if someone else can help me faster."

Don't force your searcher to make that choice.

To keep your paragraphs short and inviting, stick to two or three sentences per paragraph if that fits the publication. Limit each paragraph to one idea.

Create Flow

Do your words flow?

Or are they walls keeping the reader out?

Writing that flows drags readers from one word to the next.

A big part of that is understanding what the reader cares

about. We've taken care of that with research (KR, CA, SMA).

But another big part of that is flow.

Every sentence needs to sell the reader on the next.

That starts with your H1.

The second you give Alice a door to walk out of, she'll use it.

Here's an example of writing that flows. It's from a marketing resume guide I wrote for Zety. It's from the introduction. Notice it uses bold print, short paragraphs, and bullet lists:

We're about to make a great marketing resume, but first:

Say hello to Carolyn. She's the CEO of a Fortune 500 company that treats its marketing staff like gold. Long vacations. Flexible schedule. Great pay.

And she's hiring.

You really want to work for Carolyn.

Trouble is, you're just one of 600 electronic marketing resumes on her computer. She doesn't even know you exist.

How can you get her attention?

Better yet, how can you prove you're the next Seth Godin or Rand Fishkin?

You can do it by proving you were born to work this job.

And you were. You just need a resume that sells it.

This guide will show you:

- *A marketing resume example better than 9 out of 10 other resumes.*
- *How to write a marketing resume that will land you more interviews.*
- *Tips and examples of how to put skills and achievements on a marketing resume.*
- *How to describe your experience on a resume for marketing to get any job you want.*

Make it Pretty

One last piece of advice for stopping skimmers:

Make your article look pretty.

How does your content look when you scroll through it? Messy? Daunting? Or inviting?

Believe it or not, layout matters.

Poorly-organized content with vastly different section sizes and paragraph sizes *looks* hard to read and sloppy. It sends an unwritten message that you didn't take the time to do things right.

There are hundreds of examples of bad layout online. Not to pick on any one person or business, I chose the SEC for the screenshot below. It's from a search for "save money for college." (It came from page 7 of the Google results. Go figure.)

There will likely be restrictions on any 529 plan you may be considering. Before you invest in a 529 plan, you should read the plan's offering circular to make sure that you understand and are comfortable with any plan restrictions.

Investments. Education savings plans have certain pre-set investment options. It is not permitted to switch freely among the options. Under current tax law, an account holder is only permitted to change his or her investment option twice per year or when there is a change in the beneficiary.

Withdrawals. With limited exceptions, you can only withdraw money that you invest in an education savings plan for qualified higher education expenses or tuition for elementary or secondary schools without incurring taxes and penalties. Beneficiaries of prepaid tuition plans may only use their purchased credits or units at participating colleges or universities. If a beneficiary doesn't attend a participating college or university, the prepaid tuition plan may pay less than if the beneficiary attended a participating college or university. It may only pay a small return on the original investment.

Does investing in a 529 plan impact financial aid eligibility?

While each educational institution may treat assets held in a 529 account differently, investing in a 529 plan will generally impact a student's eligibility to receive need-based financial aid for college. You may also need to consider how having money in your 529 account for future qualified higher education expenses might affect financial aid for your student's elementary or secondary school tuition. For many families, the larger part of a financial aid package may be in loans. So, the more you can save for school, the less debt you or your student may have to incur.

Where can I find more information?

Offering Circulars for 529 Plans. You can find out more about a particular 529 plan by reading its offering circular. The National Association of State Treasurers created the College Savings Plan Network, which provides links to most 529 plan websites.

529 Expense Analyzer. 529 education savings plans have fees and expenses that can vary widely from plan to plan. The Financial Industry Regulatory Authority (FINRA) has developed a tool to help you compare how these fees and expenses can reduce returns.

Underlying Mutual Funds or Exchange-Traded Funds. Additional information about a mutual fund or ETF that is an investment option in an education savings plan is available in its prospectus, statement of additional information, and semiannual and annual shareholder reports. You can obtain these documents from the plan manager for no charge. You can also review these documents on the SEC's EDGAR database.

Fees and Expenses. You can read about the impact fees and expenses have on your investment portfolios in the SEC's Office of Investor Education and Advocacy's Investor Bulletin: How Fees and Expenses Affect Your Investment Portfolio.

(Source: SEC.gov)

That's painful. It makes me think, "ick, I'm not smart enough to read all this on my lunch break. Maybe right after breakfast I could tackle it."

Make your article as inviting as you can. Make your sections roughly the same length if possible. Break up your text with bullet lists and images at regular intervals.

When the skimmer scrolls through, your work should look as inviting as the air-conditioned lobby of a high-end business.

Here's the #1 result for the same search:

SAVING

The Best Way to Start Saving for College

⏱ 6 MINUTE READ

How much student loan debt do you think the average college student racks up by the time they cross the graduation stage? $5,000–10,000? Think again. According to the Wall Street Journal, the average college graduate's student loan debt is at a whopping $37,172. And that's just the average!

The most recent data from the Federal Reserve Bank of New York shows the overall student loan debt in America hovering just over $1.3 trillion. billion!

At this rate, college graduates will be lucky to have their student loans paid off before their kids start college! As a parent, you're probably thinking there has to be another way. Well, there is! You can start saving for college by opening a college fund. It's not easy, but with focused dedication, hard work, and careful planning, it's possible to save enough so your child can go through college debt-free!

When Should You Start Saving for College?

Saving for college is Baby Step 5, and we generally advise parents to start saving for college as soon as they can. But a lot of times it's a bit more complicated than that.

Starting a college fund is a great goal, but it's not the only goal. You likely have other financial priorities like paying off your mortgage, your credit card bill, or your own student loan debt.

You don't want to neglect your own money goals, especially when it comes to retirement savings. There are other ways to pay for college, like through grants or scholarships. Bottom line, you need to take care of your future first.

Before you can start saving for your children's college fund, it's important you've already done the following:

- Paid off any debt (this includes things like your credit card debt, your own student loan debt, etc.)
- Set up an emergency fund of 3 to 6 months of expenses to cover any unexpected costs
- Put 15% of your income toward retirement savings through your employer sponsored retirement plan, like a 401(k) and/or a Roth IRA

The Best Ways to Start a College Fund

Dave recommends saving for your children's college using the following three tax-favored plans:

Education Savings Account (ESA) or Education IRA

An ESA allows you to save $2,000 (after tax) per year, per child. Plus, it grows tax-free! If you start when your child is born and save $2,000 a year for 18 years, you would only invest $36,000. While the rate of growth will vary based on the investments in the account, you'll likely earn a much higher rate of return with an ESA than you would in a regular savings account — and you won't have to pay taxes when you withdraw the money to pay for education expenses.

Why We Like It:

- Variety of investment options
- Grows tax-free

Why We Don't:

- You must be within the income limit to qualify
- Contributions are limited to $2,000 per year
- The amount must be used by the beneficiary by age 30

529 Plan

If you want to save more for your children's college education, or if you don't meet the income limits for an ESA, then a 529 Plan could be a better option. Look for a 529 Plan that allows you to choose the funds you invest in through the account. Dave warns against using a 529 Plan that would freeze your options or automatically change your investments based on the age of your child.

The right 529 Plan will also give you the option to change the beneficiary to another family member. So if your firstborn decides not to go the college route, you can still use the funds you saved for the next kid in line.

Why We Like It:

- Higher contribution rates (varies by state, but generally you can contribute up to $300,000)

Jump-Start Your Journey   Start Now

(Source: DaveRamsey.com)

See that?

It's got clear headings with keywords in them, sections of uniform length, and bullet lists. I could read that while my two-year-old is asking me repeatedly if I can find his red robot.

Other Skim-Stoppers

Here are two more tips before we wrap up our chapter on empathy through better structure:

Write longer image captions. Readers tend to skip short captions. Sentences 2–3 sentences in length are more inviting. Why? They don't look like obvious fluff. They look like they give vital information. Of course, you then need to pack your image captions with useful information for the reader will see right through you.

Finally, try numbering your H2s. Numbered H2s tell skimmers there's a flow and that the content isn't just word salad.

That's the skinny on better structure. Set your structure up to salve the reader's pain, and Google will reward you.

Next up: a short word on including images, videos, quotes, and examples.

CHAPTER 12: ADD IMAGES, QUOTES, TWEETS, EXAMPLES, AND VIDEOS

Which do you like more?

A wall of words? Or an article with rich content that jazzes up your brain?

Old-style magazine editors knew their content wasn't books. They added sidebars, pull quotes, photos, cartoons, graphics, graphs, and other visualizations to perk up their written words.

Even a magazine for educated folk like *The New Yorker* has cartoons.

Let's reiterate the goal:

We want more traffic. To get that we need higher rankings. To get those we need searchers to stay with us and turn into readers.

If we give more bang for their buck, they'll reward us with high dwell-times.

But—

We can't just slap in any images, quotes, or videos and call it good.

Come back to your empathy and research.

What does *this reader* care most about?

With every article you publish, you're trying to make a case. You're trying to give the best advice and information possible.

Add visuals, quotes, and examples that help you drive your points home.

Images

Does every article need images? Nope. Here's the #1 Google result for "how to get a scholarship:"

That's just words and headings. Why? Probably because the writer (Ramit Sethi) knew he didn't need images to get his points across or show his reader they'd picked the right article.

It's certainly a lot better than the use of images in this piece:

ARE LATTES FATTENING?

An offshoot of the fattening coffee question, lattes do ramp up the calorie count. That's because lattes often dump in milk, sugar and flavored syrups. If we could take a centrifuge and separate out just the coffee from the latte, the result would be a low calorie (if flavorless) diet beverage.

That said, the average latte has about 150 calories. That's because they use foamed milk for a creamy taste without a creamy fat-load. Cutting out the sugar can make a latte even more diet-friendly.

Via: DailyCoffeeNews.com

IS COFFEE BAD FOR YOU ON A DIET?

Coffee isn't a terrible diet food. The caffeine in coffee can spin up the metabolism to high fat-burning levels. One downside is, diets themselves aren't the greatest idea. Short-term dieting makes us hungry and lowers our energy reserves.

In the long term, healthy eating habits like choosing fresh veggies and lean protein beat diets any day

That's not awful. It's from an article I wrote years ago. Someone who skims that article knows from the image that the article is about coffee. But that info was already in the H1 and H2s. So why add the image?

I tend not to use those kinds of images anymore. I avoid generic "fluff" pics that relate to the content but don't add information.

The key with images? They should make your skimmer think: "Oh. Already I learned something useful that relates directly to my search. Just by glancing at that image."

If your images don't do that, cut them.

One of the writers I coach does a great job adding useful images. Recently he wrote a piece for business owners and HR managers about how to turbocharge recruitment. He put this image near the top from Statista:

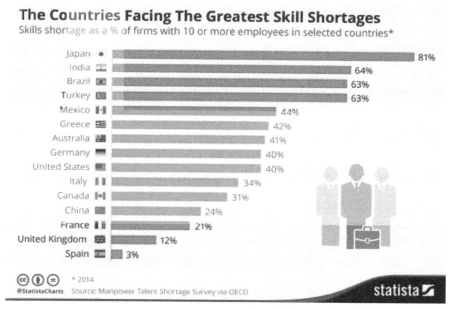

Far from fluff, that image adds extra info for the business leader wondering how to find employees, fast.

Skitch

One helpful (maybe overused) tool for adding useful images is Skitch. It's a desktop app (no longer updated for PC, but it still works there). It lets you take screenshots and mark them up with ease:

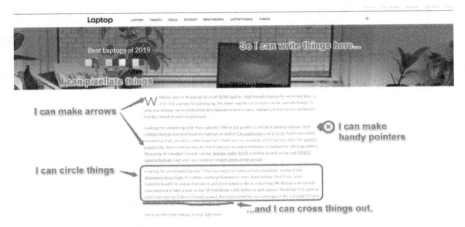

(Source: LaptopMag.com)

It's a really slick, fun tool for driving home your point with screenshots. Like other tools, it won't fit in every site.

Infogr.am

This is the best tool I've found to make aesthetically-pleasing data visualizations that work well on tiny mobile screens.

I made the graphic below in about 5 minutes with Infogr.am. For two years I used it to make 1–3 data visualizations per article. I'm convinced it helped my SEO immeasurably by getting skimmers to stop skimming and start engaging with my content.

The image below was for an article on how much money Walmart makes in a year. It shows how Walmart stacks up against the top 11 world governments by annual revenue:

Top 12 World Economies by Revenue

★ ★ ★ ★ ★

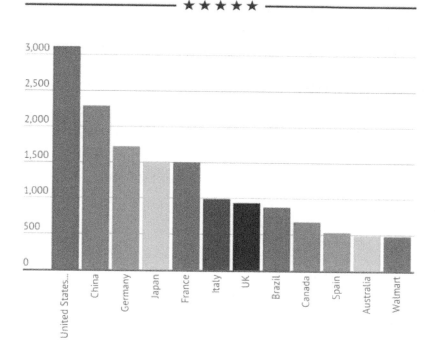

Revenue shown above is in billions of US dollars. Countries show tax revenue. Walmart shows sales revenue.

MoneyNation.com

Notice that I didn't just add this image for the sake of adding images. I gave the reader something she didn't already have. I created new information and displayed it in a new and interesting way. I didn't just say, here's how much Walmart makes in a year. I showed my reader that if Walmart were a country it would be the number 12 country in the world by revenue. That digs into my reader's emotions. It's like John Lennon says about the media: they love to turn you on. (And never mind that Lennon himself made a large fortune out of turning people on every day for decades.)

Canva is another popular online tool for making data visualizations, charts, graphs, and infographics. I confess I find it harder to use and more time consuming than Infogr.am.

Smartphones

In a pinch, you can even use your smartphone to create info-packed images. Just take a screenshot, then use your phone's built-in markup to draw and comment on the image.

Here's an image I made from the text of this book just now with my iPhone:

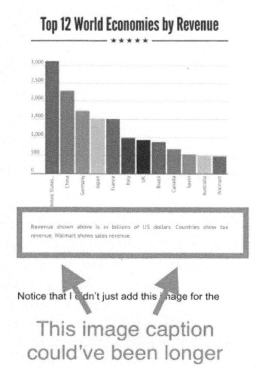

Tweets & Instagram

It's easy and kind of fun to embed ready-made tweets and Instagram posts into your content. Again the key is relevance.

Does the embedded content add value for the reader? Will it blow the reader's hair back or give necessary info? Then include it.

Here's a screenshot of an embedded tweet about embedded tweets.

Just click the little drop-down menu on the right side of any tweet, then select "Embed Tweet" to get the HTML code. You can paste it into most WordPress posts and it'll pop the tweet right into your content. If that doesn't work, you can always take a screenshot of the tweet, but I have a sneaking suspicion Google rates your relevance higher if you embed tweets with related keywords. Again, not necessarily because *Google* likes the keywords, but because the reader sees them and knows the tweets relate to what she's searching.

Instagram embeds work the same way.

Videos

Embedded videos can boost a reader's dwell time too.

In 2015 I wrote an article about NBA Salary. I did a quick search on YouTube and found a video by BuzzFeed that compared NBA players to regular people. (Kobe Bryant earns as much as 959 nurses. That's about 90% of the entire nursing budget of Los Angeles County.)

For more about how NBA salary compares to others, check out our article, "How Much are You Worth Compared to an NBA Player?"

Chances of Earning an NBA Salary

What are the chances of earning an NBA salary? Not good. The chances are just .03%, or one in 3,000. That doesn't mean one of every 3,000 people is an NBA player. That number is more like one in a million. What it means is that only one in every 3,000 people who really try to be an NBA player will make it.

Compared to other careers, someone who tries to be a doctor or lawyer is 400 times more likely to succeed than someone who goes for an NBA salary. Nurse candidates are 1,100 times more likely to succeed. Teachers are 1,167 times more likely to make it.

The odds of becoming the president of the United States are

That's nice, but it would've worked better if I'd left out the clipart under the next heading.

Embedding relevant videos that help solve the reader's problem can keep them with you longer—especially since a single click will play the video directly from your page.

But even if your reader—Alice—doesn't watch the videos, she knows they're there to help her. She can see from the image that the video pertains directly to her question.

Also, keep videos short. Most internet users won't watch anything longer than five minutes.

Quotes

Quotes (or pull quotes) are another way to show readers you care.

How do they help SEO?

They add credibility at a glance.

A Nielsen study shows 85% of readers trust content from experts more than "plain ol'" writers.

Quotes from experts that back up your points tell readers, "You're in the right place."

Most WordPress themes let users add pull quotes (also known as callouts or block quotes).

Pull quotes draw the eye. Put keywords in them, and your reader knows she didn't take a wrong turn somewhere.

Here's a good example from an article on pull quotes from CreativePro.com:

right now is not a no-brainer. In some areas home prices may fall further. If you own a house now, it may take longer than you expect to sell it, and you may walk away with less cash than you thought. "It's a good time to buy, but it's still a really difficult market," says Patrick Newport of IHS Global Insight. As the clock ticks toward the tax-credit deadline, answer these questions to decide whether

32%

buyers can get up to $8,000). But according to the National Association of Realtors, buyers spend about

Metropolitan areas where home prices at the end of September 2010 are expected to be at least 5% lower than the previous year.

source: [...]

eight years. The good news: Once you've signed the contract, you have until June 30 to close the deal.

A dramatic treatment that highlights important information in red can be a convincing marketing technique. *Money* magazine.

Aside from stopping skimmers, quotes from experts can add

real value to your piece. They also take very little time and effort to get. As I said in an earlier chapter, it's as easy as finding someone with something to sell. (A professor with a book out or a government or nonprofit agency trying to get their message out.) I like to fire off a few emails fast, then use any quotes that come back in.

And of course there's always HARO (Help A Reporter Out). It's a way to post a question to hundreds of thousands of sources and get quotes back fast. Though to be honest, HARO generates a healthy whack of spam with every query.

There's another big way to show your reader that you've got her back. It's with lots of reader comments. That's next.

CHAPTER 13: GET COMMENTS TO PROVE YOU'LL MEET THE READER'S NEEDS

Why do reader comments help with SEO?

Well—

Why do people go on cruise ships?

In January of 2012, the 114,147-ton cruise ship *Costa Concordia* ran smack into a reef near Tuscany. 32 passengers were killed and 64 were injured. The rest certainly didn't have the vacation of a lifetime. Thousands of articles online and in print trumpeted the disaster around the world. There are even several books about it on Amazon.

Cruise ships get attacked by pirates. They run aground, catch fire, and flood. Then there's the notorious norovirus—an acute gastrointestinal illness that attacks tens of thousands of passengers per year.

If we could generate power from bad press about cruise ships, we could solve the world's clean energy needs.

Yet 20 million people a year take cruises, according to TripSavvy.com.

Why?

If cruises have such so much bad press, then why do people continue to flock to them like they're the secret to eternal life?

Cruises also get their fair share of good press. I'm not talking about travel magazines, though those almost certainly help. I'm talking about Facebook, Twitter, and Instagram.

The #cruiseship hashtag on Instagram has over a million posts. Many have thousands of engagements. The hashtag #cruise has over *seven* million. Then there's:

- #Cruising
- #CruiseLife
- #Cruises
- #Cruiser

And (if you're interested) about 50 others, not to mention all the line-specific and ship-specific ones like #CarnivalCruise or #CruiseNorwegian.

How many times per year do people post on social media about cruises? Tens of millions? Hundreds of millions? Billions?

Whatever the figure, when people go on cruises, they love to post about it. Nobody ever posts an image of sitting at their desk looking haggard, maybe drooling a little on an expense report. But boy howdy, we love to share our fun times, don't we? Social media is like the highlights reel for our lives. Even if we only go on a single cruise in five years, you can bet we'll slather pictures of it all over the socialverse.

How can negative media compete with that?

How can a million or so articles about the dangers and frustrations of cruises fight a tidal wave of images of people eating steak and lobster claws or snorkeling in water the color of Aqua-Velva?

They can't.

On top of that, pile the word-of-mouth advertising cruises

generate.

People flock to cruises for the same reason they flock to Disneyworld. Social proof says everybody loves them.

Social proof in marketing is nothing new. Robert Cialdini's 1984 book *Influence* devotes an entire chapter to it. He covers studies that show:

- Laugh tracks on sitcoms convince audiences jokes are funnier.
- Cults use social proof to convert skeptics. (The common if insensitive business-term "drink the Kool-Aid" comes directly from this tactic.)
- In emergencies, social proof can influence bystanders to ignore people in need.

Marketing agencies have made good use of social proof for years.

Amazon does it. On the fence about whether you should buy Cialdini's book? Just look at Amazon's little 5-star review graphic. 2,076 satisfied readers can't be wrong.

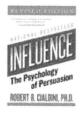
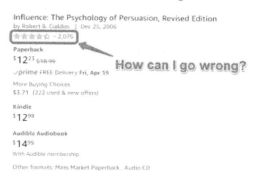

Influence: The Psychology of Persuasion, Revised Edition
by Robert B. Cialdini | Dec 26, 2006

★ ★ ★ ★ ☆ ~ 2,076

Paperback
$12²³ $18.99
✓prime FREE Delivery Fri, Apr 19

How can I go wrong?

More Buying Choices
$3.71 (222 used & new offers)

Kindle
$12⁹⁹

Audible Audiobook
$14⁹⁵
With Audible membership

Other formats: Mass Market Paperback , Audio CD

(Source: Amazon.com)

I ran afoul of social proof myself when, at the tender age of 20, I took a job canvassing neighborhoods in Massachusetts, soliciting donations for a political action group.

My supervisor reminded me of Fagin from *Oliver*. He had a million tricks to get people to donate.

One of his favorites was social proof. "Tell them their neighbors are being really helpful," he said. "Tell them it's overwhelming how much money they're shelling out. Even if it's the first person in the neighborhood you talk to."

I did well at that job, but I quit after a few weeks because it made me feel dirty. To this day, when a sales rep tells me how excited my neighbors are about a product, I shut down.

As dirty as it was in that case, it makes sense to take our cues from legitimate instances of social proof. If lots of people like us are doing something, it's a safe bet that it might be good for us, too.

In the 1980s, anti-drug ads used social proof the wrong way. In Jonah Berger's book, *Contagious: Why Things Catch On*, Berger references anti-marijuana ads that showed "cool kids" smoking marijuana. According to Berger:

"In fact, the messages actually seemed to increase drug use. Kids aged twelve and a half to eighteen who saw the ads were actually more likely to smoke marijuana. Why? Because it made drug use more public. Think about observability and social proof. Before seeing the message, some kids might never have thought about taking drugs. Others might have considered it but have been wary about doing the wrong thing. But anti-drug ads often say two things simultaneously. They say that drugs are bad, but they also say that other people are doing them. And as we've discussed throughout this chapter, the more others seem to be doing something, the more likely people are to think that thing is right or normal and what they should be doing as well."

More recently, anti-drug campaigners seem to have learned from their mistakes. I spoke with Dr. Cynthia Kuhn recently, Duke University brain science researcher and author of *Just Say Know: Talking With Kids About Drugs and Alcohol*. She says one of the most effective ways to protect kids from drugs is to share statistics about how *few* of their peers are doing them.

Use Comments as Social Proof

A few years ago I got a firsthand lesson in the power of reader comments as a social-proof-based SEO tool.

It was Christmas 2016. Hoverboards were everywhere. They were the gift that caused Black Friday stampedes. Every parent who could afford one *had to get one* for his child.

But then they started catching fire.

Being a mercenary hack for a money blog, I tried to think how to get traffic from the tragedy while still providing value.

So, I wrote an article called "How to Get Your Money Back for a Hoverboard."

True to my habit of creating value, I didn't write a fluff piece. I did my research—KR, CA, SMA. I found out it was really hard to get a refund for a hoverboard. Many companies denied their hoverboards had problems. Hundreds of thousands of shoppers found themselves frustrated, stonewalled by retailers.

So I did some outreach. I called retailers, manufacturers, and the U.S. Consumer Product Safety Commission (CPSC). I got the lowdown on which hoverboards should be returned. I covered all aspects of returns and laid my readers' rights out plainly. The situation was confusing, but I managed to make sense of it. The article ranked #1 in days.

Then something magical happened. The piece got 91 reader comments. Many were a few hundred words long. Suddenly the text in my article grew five or six times in size—from 2,000 words to 20,000. And all of it was laced with relevant keywords.

Here's why that's important:

The site went bust a couple years later. The site's owner stopped adding new articles. All the old articles vanished from the rankings. Traffic dropped from 600,000 a month to 200,000 to 50,000 to zilch. The site sunk without a trace.

But not that article. It became the article that would not die. Years later, when all the other 750+ articles on the site have long since foundered in the mire of SEO hell, that one article keeps chugging.

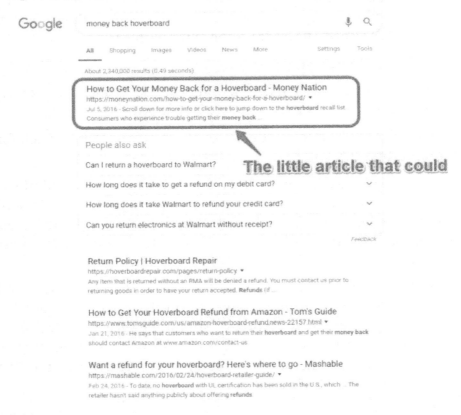

(Source: Google.com)

How can this be? How can a site with an Alexa rank of 1 million and low Domain Authority beat sites with DA in the 90s? Especially when none of its other articles rank at all, for anything?

To paraphrase James Carville—

It's the comments, stupid!

Those 91 comments packed with keywords, all generated by users, made the difference.

Why?

First, readers stay with the page longer because they *read* the comments. They also read the article more carefully, guessing that if 91 people had a lively discussion about it, the article must have valuable info.

Second, the comments have dates. The longer the comments kept coming, the more recent the dates, and the more Google rated the article as timely and current.

Third, Google's algorithm may take those comments as a sign that people like the article. (There's a robust debate on this in the SEO community, but the consensus is that comments at the very least don't hurt.)

Fourth, the comments add more text. We said earlier that size doesn't matter, but that's not true when it comes to comments. A study by SERPIQ shows the top five results in Google usually run longer than the second five.

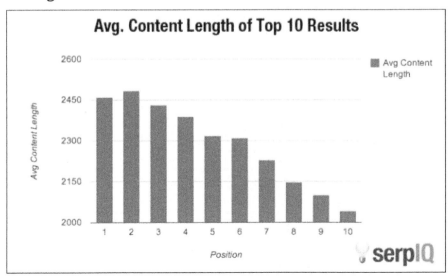

Doesn't that go against the idea that readers don't always want long posts?

Well—they don't necessarily want to *read* long posts. But readers know the comment section is optional. They can skip it. But they know it means the article has crowd appeal.

Do comments really help SEO? The debate rages, but here's some evidence they do:

- Blogging site Copyblogger yanked comments from their site in 2014. After two years they brought them back again.
- Popular blogger Michael Hyatt pulled comments from his blog too—then put them back a year later.
- Blogger Harsh Agrawal disabled comments to his blog and saw his traffic drop by 40%. When he reinstated comments, his traffic rebounded instantly.

Some SEO gurus say comments don't influence SEO much. In a 2011 study, marketing site HubSpot found no relationship between number of comments and number of post views.

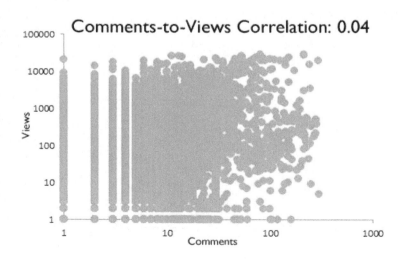

Likewise, SEO guru Neil Patel questions the value of comments, though he does agree they drive at least some traffic. (He estimates that 16% of all his search traffic comes from comments.)

But I keep coming back to that hoverboard article. It's got zero backlinks. It's got earthworm-level Page Authority and Domain Authority. Every other article of the 750+ on the site now fails to rank. But that one sticks like super glue.

I believe the article's success is largely thanks to comments.

But come back to our goal—to think like Google and to serve the reader. Comments are at the very least a great way to show the Reader that our article is the right one to read. If our articles have lots of comments, the reader knows we think like Google. The reader knows we have the most appeal of any article out there.

But how do we get more comments?

How to Get More Comments

Sometimes you feel like a voice crying out in the wilderness.

You bleed from your forehead to put words on the screen. You create Herculean masses of glittering content.

You may get traffic or you may not.

But no one comments.

Are you missing something? Doing something wrong?

Well, let's take a tip from Neil Patel.

Patel routinely gets hundreds of comments on every post he writes.

(Source: NeilPatel.com)

He doesn't get all those comments by accident. Nor do other content creators who pile up 100–300 comments per post.

Without further preamble, here are 14 ways to get more comments:

1. You're Already Doing This One

The best way to get lots of comments is with the tools I've already shared.

Know your reader's problem, and her pain. Tap into her emotions—fear, failure, success, joy, excitement, anger, or frustration. Create massive value no one else is giving. Give better advice and information that runs counter to what everyone is saying.

Do those things and you'll rank high. You'll get more traffic. Your words will resonate with readers, and they'll comment more.

At Zety, we work hard to provide a *ton* of value with every post. We bend over backwards to write engaging articles that serve the searcher more than any of the competition. We also answer every single comment. Thanks to all that effort, we get a lot of comments. That ultimately helps our SEO.

(Source: Zety.com)

Now let's move on to a few things you're *not* already doing:

2. Ask for Comments With Open-Ended Questions

Sometimes admitting there's no answer can be more powerful than answers.

When I wrote my hoverboard article, I hit some dead ends. Laws varied by state. Some retailers were salty. Some compan-

Can't fix everything? Don't sweat it. Leave open-ended questions at the end of your articles. Use them to ask for comments. Make them emotional, because that's motivational.

What's an open-ended question?

Let's start with some closed-ended ones. They have one-word answers. Here are five:

Closed-Ended Questions	
Do you like ice cream?	Yes.
What color are your eyes?	Blue.
What's your favorite TV show?	Knight Rider.
How many fingers am I holding up?	Three.
Do you have a dog?	Yes.

Those questions are boring. They have short-answers. They don't spark discussion. Nobody wants to comment on them. Why not? Because they don't let us show off our individuality.

Now look at the next list. The questions are open-ended. They're a soapbox for the reader. They say, "Tell us what you think. We want to know."

Open-Ended Questions	
What kind of relationship do you have with your boss?	
What do you find frustrating about applying for jobs online?	
What makes you angry about the President?	
What was the best movie in history?	
What are your goals for the next five years?	
What's the craziest thing your dog ever did?	
What's your proudest business moment?	

Open-ended questions spark conversation, especially if the reader knows you value her opinions.

When job seekers ask me how to get referrals, I say the first thing is to connect with employers. But don't do it by asking for a job. Do it by asking about *their* jobs. That's because nobody has five seconds to listen to you ask for help. But everyone has an hour to talk about how great they are.

People love to talk about themselves. Give them permission and a forum and they'll do it gladly.

In an article about investing you could ask:

- What's your biggest frustration with investing? Tell us in a comment.
- What will you do when you reach your investing goals? Let us know!
- Should you focus more on growth or value? Tell us below.

3. Ask for Help

People love to give advice.

In *The Alchemist,* Paulo Coelho says, "Everyone seems to have a clear idea of how other people should lead their lives, but none about his or her own."

When Kathy was pregnant with our first child, we could have written a book on parenting from all the unsolicited advice we got. It got so pervasive I complained, "Most of these people have one or two kids. They're hardly experts. It's like if I made a cheeseburger and became convinced I was Ronald McDonald."

Psychologist Leon Seltzer says we give advice to feel powerful and boost our self-esteem.

Whatever the reason, asking for advice is a tried and tested way to generate a pile of comments.

In a food magazine, you could whip up comments with questions like:

- I bet my editor $50 that more people like corned beef

than roast beef. He says I'm crazy. Help us settle it! Leave your fav in a comment.

- This is the best cheesecake recipe I've found, but we wish there was a way to do it faster without cracking. Can you help? Leave a comment.
- Edge cut? Center cut? We can't decide. Help us in the comments section.

4. Tap Influencers

Sometimes you don't have comments because you don't have traffic.

If that's you, kill two birds with one stone by tapping influencers.

Influencers are the people in your industry who *do* have traffic. They've got a ready-made audience. If you can get them interested, so will you.

There are two ways to do it:

1. Interview them.

Reach out to an influencer and ask to interview her. It works best if she's selling something, because people with a message need publicity.

If they like your content, they might tweet about it or share it on LinkedIn. A tweet like that can turn into a pile of comments.

2. Mention them.

Do you respect an influencer in your industry? Show it! Shout out his book or product with a link and say how great it is. Again, he might tweet it, and that can lead to comments.

Writer Yaro Starak knows how to call out influencers. In a post that got 29 value-packed comments on his personal blog, he mentioned writer Darren Rowse, with a link to Rowse's ProBlogger site and unabashed praise.

Do You Have What It Takes To Be A Professional Blogger?

Hi,
I'm Yaro

In the first part of this series on professional blogging as a business model I explained the content + traffic = money equation as the root formula for nearly all currently successful professional bloggers and those who are working to replicate their success.

If you have not done so already, please read the opening article here –

Is Professional Blogging A Sustainable Business Model?

Darren Rowse, A Leading Professional Blogger

I first came across Darren Rowse in 2004, and his Problogger.net blog appeared to be well put together and intriguing, but at the time I was beginning my research into blogging and was far from making any money from my own blog – in fact I didn't have any intentions of doing so. If it wasn't for one unique thing, that Darren was an Aussie from Melbourne and I am from Australia too, I would not have spent nearly as much time studying Darren and his blog as I did.

Darren has a lot to answer to in the professional blogging world. It's partly his fault that so many people currently do or are attempting to make money from blogging. If it wasn't for events like this slashdot news post in July 05 about Darren earning between $10,000 and $20,000 per month from blogging, and the countless articles, blog posts and offline newspaper features on Darren's success (he's probably seen cheques and payments at double or triple his 2005 monthly income average since then – Darren?), not quite as many would know that this whole professional blogging thing was possible.

If it wasn't Darren then no doubt some other professional blogger would have risen to spread

So how do you find influencers?

It's important to find influencers—not celebrities. Celebrities have all the press they need and then some. The media mentions them nine million times per day. You can mention Stephen King all you like in your content. He will never mention you back.

Influencers are people with big social media followings—Twitter, Instagram, LinkedIn, or Facebook. They post a lot on social media and people listen to them.

You can find them by searching Twitter, Instagram, or LinkedIn.

I just opened Twitter and did a people search for "food blogger." I instantly found dozens of bloggers with 50,000–100,000 followers and more. The same trick works for lifestyle bloggers, financial bloggers, and any other topic we can think of.

5. Make it Easy

I just read a great article on Forbes with a seven-step blueprint for retiring early.

It didn't even have one comment.

Why not?

Forbes doesn't allow reader comments on its articles. They're rethinking how to do it right (since 2017).

Other online publications serve up the dreaded "log in to comment" barrier. (Ugh. Who wants to deal with that?) Still others make you click on all the pictures that have street signs in them or hills or mountains.

Captchas, logins, and disallowing reader comments don't help SEO. If you can spare the time, allow them and make them easy. Afraid of spam? WordPress and the Disqus community platform both have great spam blockers.

6. Respond

Here's the fastest way to stop discussion on your articles:

Don't be part of it.

Readers notice when you answer other commenters. (Google may too.)

In the image near the top of this section, did you notice Neil Patel actually *responds* to reader comments?

Respond to every comment, and readers will know their words won't hit a brick wall.

Need other ways to get reader comments? You can send bulk emails to your subscriber list or say something controversial in your article.

Neil Patel wrote an excellent piece with 25 ways to get more comments on your content. You can read it here.

Now you know how to show the searcher you've done your homework. You know how to serve your editor and deliver better information. You've seen how to write more engaging introductions, cut the fat, and write better-structured content.

You know to stuff your articles with examples, images, quotes, and videos when you can and when they're helpful. Finally, you know how to get more comments to prove to readers that you empathize with them.

But proving that to readers is only part of the equation.

We also have to prove our empathy to Google.

PART 5: PROVE TO GOOGLE THAT YOU'RE DOING IT

CHAPTER 14: PROVE EMPATHY THROUGH BETTER BACKLINKS

There are ways to prove to Google that you've done your homework and rank higher.

In Part 1, we said that to rank, we need to feel the reader's pain.

In Part 2, we saw how to do that with research into keywords, other articles, and social media.

In part 3, we learned to show we care, so the reader sees it at a glance and sticks around.

Now it's time to prove to Google that we do it *well*.

The most powerful way is backlinks.

But be warned:

Backlinks are a bugbear.

Remember how we said keywords aren't the shining star of SEO anymore?

They were at first. Google's algorithm used them to decide which pages served the reader best. Then black-hatters—people trying to trick Google—stuffed their content with keywords until Google changed its algorithm.

Google's first foray away from keywords was backlinks.

The reasoning went like this: The better a piece of content is, the more other pages will link to it.

Google's algorithm started ranking pages higher if they had lots of inbound links. (That's the basis for Google's PageRank score from Chapter 11 and Moz's Domain Authority from Chapter 5).

But the black-hatters didn't give up. They changed their strategy and started building links.

For years, everyone's favorite SEO strategy was, "build as many links as possible."

People started buying and selling links. Link farms sprouted up across the digital landscape. Thousands of articles appeared, teaching content creators how to build more links.

One of the most popular ways to build links was to reach out to other content creators and ask for them.

Predictably, Google noticed this too. They don't like it when people trick their algorithm by building lots of artificial links. If Google's goal is to identify the best articles, then building links isn't thinking like Google. It's thinking like a scammer. Do it, and you'll rank high—until Google rolls out a new update and shakes you off.

To do that, Google started *ranking* links. Links from sites with low DA (like *Jimmy Bob's Business and Meat Snack Blog*) have little power. Links from high DA sites (like *Forbes* or *CNN*) have lots.

Some SEO pros call it "link juice." Moz uses the more hygienic term "link equity."

Google's new reasoning goes like this:

Prestigious sites like *Forbes* and *HuffPost* don't sell links. They link to content because it's valuable—not because somebody paid them $50. So if Google tweaks its rankings based on whether *quality* sites link to your content, they'll know which articles are best.

Want proof? Google gives it right in its terms of service.

(Source: Google.com)

Putting it baldly, Google *hates* link-building. It hates it almost as much as it hates building articles around keywords. You shouldn't do it. Not because you're the content-creating equivalent of Mother Teresa, but because it doesn't work.

Even when it does work, it still doesn't work. What's that mean? It isn't future-proof. Google always figures out new ways to soak the black hatters.

In spite of that, there are *all kinds of ultimate guides to link-building* out there on the internet, just waiting to convince you to do it anyway.

They'll tell you to find sites already linking to content like yours, then reach out to them. "Hey," they'll tell you to say, "I noticed you linked to XYZ site's guide on parrot training. It's a really good article. But I've just written a 10X ultimate guide to parrot training that I think you'll LOVE! Why not link to it? Here's the link! PS—if you link to me I'll link to you."

Yeah, don't do that.

Google considers that a link-building scheme. If they find out, they'll fire a nuclear SEO bomb at your site and ducking and covering won't help.

So—if we're not allowed to build links to our pages, how can we get links ethically?

It can be done. It's not that hard.

Case in point:

With my 750 articles on the money site I worked for, I landed 8,949 backlinks. Many were from sites like HuffPost, the *BBC*, *NBC*, and *Forbes*, with DAs in the 80s and 90s.

Full disclosure: I *think* the site owner did some outreach and link-building work. He never said.

But whether he did or not, he wasn't building links with those high DA sites I just mentioned. He wasn't calling *Forbes* and saying, "Hey guys, could you link to me?" They would have laughed him off the phone.

Yet still my articles managed 8,949 backlinks from high-authority sites.

(Source: Ahrefs.com)

With about 750 articles, that's an average of 12 per page. (It's actually a lot higher than that, because I didn't know what I was doing for at least the first six months.)

Here's a short list of the publications that linked to us:

- Wikipedia
- VanityFair
- Cheatsheet
- Politifact
- Refinery29
- Salon
- Hubspot
- BleacherReport
- TheSun
- MensHealth
- Cosmopolitan
- The Daily Beast
- NBC News
- HuffingtonPost
- Investopedia
- TheStreet
- Mic
- IBTimes
- Medium
- Bustle
- Blogging.org
- TheBlaze
- SFGate
- Forbes
- Princeton.edu
- TheRichest
- TheWrap
- DailyWire
- LifeHack
- Breitbart
- CNBC
- The BBC

- Screenrant

Keep in mind, this was one guy (okay, with the occasional article from the site owner or the editor) getting all these links. Again, we had no special deals with any of these publications.

So how did we do it? Without using all the crazy backlink-building schemes the SEO wonks recommend, how did we build nearly 9,000 high-quality backlinks in essentially 18 months?

How to Build Backlinks so Google Doesn't Hate You

It turns out there's a great, approved way to build backlinks.

The best part? You don't have to do anything special.

Just do what I've already outlined so far in this book.

Remember that the site that got those 8,900 backlinks in 18 months was nothing when it started. It had six articles. It had an ocean-bottom Domain Authority (I think it was 25).

To get that kind of backlink explosion from a nothing site (or any site) you just need to follow the simple steps I've outlined in earlier chapters.

That is:

Think like Google. Build reader empathy through KR, CA, and SMA. Understand the reader's problem. Work to solve that problem. Find a way to do that better than anyone else.

Create that kind of unique value, and you'll get links. Lots of them.

Let's look at how it works. It's a bit of a chicken-and-egg scenario. I wrote it as a numbered list, but in truth it all evolves at the same time:

1. Build reader empathy. Write unique articles that really help.

2. Rank high (because you wrote unique articles that understood the reader's needs, and because the reader loved them).

3. Get noticed by the big fish because you're at the top of the results.

4. Get links from the big fish because you created something unique and they can tell. They link to you because they want to use your awesome facts, advice, or structure and they can't get it anywhere else.

Build that better mousetrap and you'll get the links.

Backlinks: A Case Study

In July of 2016, gaming company Niantic had an idea. They made a video game that used a player's smartphone camera to "see" otherwise invisible game characters in the real world. Aim your phone at your fireplace or a street corner, and you might see a "Bulbasaur" or "Charmander" perched there, offering to fight you.

The game was an overnight success. Within weeks it had 310 million downloads. Within seven days of its release, Nintendo's stock price jumped by 57% or $9.7 billion. A few days later investors realized their mistake—Nintendo didn't make Pokemon Go. A company called Niantic did. Nintendo owns 33% of Niantic. Even so, the stock only lost 21% in the correction. It maintained a 36% gain or $7.7 billion.

Yet everyone online was saying Niantic could hope to make as much as half a billion a year in revenue from Pokemon Go.

Something was very wrong. I did some analyzing. A rough rule of thumb for valuation says a company is worth about 10 years of revenue. Well, 10 years at half a billion a year is $5 billion. Not to get too detailed, Nintendo's 33% of $5 billion should be $1.65 billion. Not $7 billion.

Had investors gone crazy? What was going on here?

I decided to find out. I set out to build a better mousetrap that would show my readers exactly what was happening.

First, Pokemon Go was insanely popular. The Super Bowl gets 125 million viewers, yet in 2016 a 30-second Super Bowl ad cost $5 million. (That's how much the air time costs. It doesn't include the cost to make the ad.)

In just a few weeks, Pokemon Go already had twice as many active users as the Super Bowl. And those viewers weren't just tuning in for one night. They were playing multiple times *every day.*

That's a lot of eyeball time. I made a little graph that showed exactly how it worked:

(Source: MoneyNation.com)

Not satisfied with that, I calculated the Super Bowl's total ad revenue for 2016 at $275 million. Extrapolating, Pokemon Go's potential annual ad revenue was in the neighborhood of $16 billion.

The other articles online had arrived at Pokemon Go's annual earnings of half a billion by estimating in-app purchases. They'd completely missed the potential ad revenue.

More importantly, I reasoned that Pokemon Go would transform the advertising world. It carried the potential to drive foot traffic to brick-and-mortar stores. The company had plans to charge businesses to become "Pokestops." (In fact those plans are now reality.)

So, instead of just placing ads from Ford or Walmart in the game, the company could charge every little convenience store and sandwich shop in the world to bring actual, physical people through the doors.

In other words, I'd built a better mousetrap. I did a deeper analysis. I showed facts nobody else was serving up.

The article ranked high in a few days and got a ton of traffic. Even better, it got 108 backlinks, including some from Huff-Post, IBTimes, and HubSpot. Again, we didn't reach out to those publications to ask for links. They just linked in on their own.

My most linked-to article though was "Hillary Clinton Net Worth" with 426 inbound links.

(Source: Ahrefs.com)

Again, those links came from looking at what everyone else was saying, then digging deeper and presenting better information in a better way. They came from doing all the things I laid out in earlier chapters of this book.

Write Linkbait

If you want people to link to you, you must create something unique and valuable.

You must become a *source*.

That means you can't parrot what everyone else is saying.

You have to dig up some gold. Create a better mousetrap.

But to do that, you need to recalibrate your empathy.

Until now, we've been working hard to manufacture empathy for searchers, skimmers, and readers.

Now we need to aim our empathy machine at other content creators.

Think hard about them. What do they want most?

They want to create great content fast.

Most of them don't have time to do a lot of research. They don't have time to create something new. They want to find something valuable that's ready made so they can share it with their readers.

That's where you come in.

If you want links, your job is to make them look gooood.

Here are five ways to make articles that draw link like a bug zapper.

1. Do Original Research

If most content creators don't have time to do research, and you do, they'll lavish you with links.

Remember the money site I worked for? We got 8,900+ links, and many were high-quality. Here's how we created something unique with research:

Many of our articles were net worth posts. Justin Bieber net worth. Tom Brady net worth. Bernie Sanders net worth.

My boss wanted me to write those articles. But when I sat down to write the first one, I noticed something irritating.

All the existing net worth articles said something like this:

Tom Brady is a quarterback for the New England Patriots. He is married to Gisele Bundchen. He has won five (now six) Super Bowl championships. He earned an NFL Salary in 2014 of $11 million. He has done endorsements for Foot Locker and Gatorade. His net worth is $135 million.

I read several of those articles six times. Once again I remembered the old guy who called in to the rock station I used to work at. *"Where do you get your information!?"*

Those net worth articles said nothing. They had no links. No sources. They didn't show their math. They just wrote a paragraph or two with some facts about a celebrity, then made up a figure. They weren't even *trying* to be accurate.

So for my first net worth piece, I opened up a Google Sheet. My celebrity was a singer, so I made a list of all her albums and singles. I found rough sales data for each. Then I found a source that said how much of the revenue a big-name singer kept from each album sale.

I added everything up and did the same for YouTube revenue, perfume sales, book sales, movie appearances, and every other income stream I could find. I estimated income by year, then did tax, expense, and investment calculations by year, too.

Then I presented all that data to my readers, along with disclaimers that my figures were estimates provided for entertainment only.

The links poured in because I'd created something nobody else had. Forbes, Fortune, The Economist, and dozens of other big-name sites linked to my articles. Why?

Because otherwise they'd have to link to sites with zero data and no sources. Anyone who read my net worth articles carefully could see exactly where I got my info.

PewDiePie Net Worth Calculations						
Year	Approx. Earnings From YouTube Views	PewDiePie Merchandising Income	Taxes	PewDiePie Portion After Tax	Expenses	PewDiePie Earnings After Tax and Expenses
2010	$7,788,415	$5,377,389	$5,924,612	$7,241,192	$100,000	$7,141,192
2011	$15,576,830	$5,377,389	$9,429,399	$11,524,820	$100,000	$11,424,820
2012	$15,576,830	$5,377,389	$9,429,399	$11,524,820	$100,000	$11,424,820
2013	$15,576,830	$5,377,389	$9,429,399	$11,524,820	$100,000	$11,424,820
2014	$15,576,830	$5,377,389	$9,429,399	$11,524,820	$100,000	$11,424,820
2015	$15,576,830	$5,377,389	$9,429,399	$11,524,820	$100,000	$11,424,820
2016	$28,273,952	$9,510,347	$17,002,935	$20,781,365	$100,000	$20,681,365
Totals	$113,946,517	$41,774,681	$70,074,539	$85,646,659	$700,000	$84,946,659

(Source: MoneyNation.com)

Once I got used to writing articles like that, I could do all my net worth research on any celebrity in a couple hours.

Do a Study or a Survey

Original research can also be a study or a survey.

Sound daunting?

It doesn't have to be.

You don't have to spend six weeks calling 2,000 business owners or ice-cream shop employees to collect enough data for a linkbait survey.

One strategy that works (and works fast) is to partner with an influencer.

Find someone in your industry with a big social media presence and reach out to them.

Ask them if they'll post for you on LinkedIn or Twitter in exchange for a link to their site or book.

When they post their question, the answers are your survey.

Pick an influencer whose posts get lots of engagement.

Here's an example:

I wanted to write an article on what to do if you just lost your job. Luckily, I knew a human resources expert who was extremely active on LinkedIn.

Every time this guy posted, he'd get 200 responses, 300 responses, sometimes 500 responses—all of them from hiring managers and recruiters.

Holy cow, I realized. What an opportunity to conduct a survey of employment experts.

So I asked if he'd post my question. He did, and got 187 responses. Not his best, he said, but not too bad. But to me it was a goldmine. In three minutes of my time I'd done a survey of 187 hiring experts. I used their responses to write an article that got one of the highest email-open rates our company had seen to date.

2. Call an Expert and Dig for an "Aha" Moment

Do anything you can to avoid being a parrot.

Parrots don't get links. Parrots get shunted to Google's sock drawer.

Don't have two hours to do massive research or a social media survey?

That's okay. A super-fast way to build something unique is by calling an expert.

If you've got expert testimony in your article, it's valuable. Content creators will link to it.

They'll link to it because they can't get it anywhere else. They'll say, "Oh, look what XYZ expert said about my topic! I don't have time to interview him. I'll just link to this great article."

But do you have time to interview an expert?

Here's the secret:

Interviewing an expert takes almost no time at all. That is, if you do it right.

Here are a few tips to tap expert knowledge fast:

1. **Start early.** Don't sit down to write your content and then think, "Hey, I ought to have an expert quote here." Reach out at least a day or two in advance.
2. **Offer a link.** Experts write books. They want to sell books. Sometimes they sell products too. Books and products have websites and Amazon links. Offering a trade will often get them to answer you.
3. **Outline first.** Before you ask your questions, do your research (KR, CA, SMA). Outline your article and have a rough idea of how your article will unfold.
4. **Keep empathy in mind.** You need to make something unique, remember? So with your questions, dig for the "aha" moment. Ask for the counterintuitive.
5. **Be flexible.** Ask if they'd rather do the interview by phone or email.
6. **If it's email, great!** This takes almost zero time. Now that you know your outline, ask your questions.
7. **If it's phone, don't fret.** Record the call with an app like TapeACall. Then upload it to Temi for cheap AI transcription that's 90% correct.
8. **Bask.** Your source's answers have already written part

of your content for you. You've also got something unique that others will be glad to link to.

I do phone interviews while I'm driving or out for a run or bike ride. That way they take zero work time, but still create unique value that other content writers love to link to.

In a great *New York Times* article, Erik Winkowski interviewed Dr. Piers Steel about procrastination. Steel is a motivational psychology professor. He's also the author of a book called, *The Procrastination Equation.*

According to Steel, procrastination isn't about self-control or laziness. It's about bad moods. We know we face a task we won't do well at. That makes us feel bad, so we avoid it.

The cure for procrastination then, doesn't have anything to do with productivity apps or deleting Facebook from your phone. It has to do with self-compassion.

That's the kind of aha moment we're looking for when we're trying to build links.

If you're curious, that post already has over 37,000 backlinks, three weeks after publication. Wow. I know it's the *Times,* but STILL.

Backlink profile for https://www.nytimes.com/2019/03/25/smarter-living/why-you-procrastinate-it-has-nothing-to-do-with-self-control.html
Exact URL

URL rating	Domain rating	Backlinks	Referring domains
46	94	37,091	913
		99% dofollow	92% dofollow

(Source: Ahrefs.com)

3. Create Something Emotional

Want an avalanche of links?

Don't have time for interviews or research?

Hit your reader in her emotions.

Remember my theory about why Donald Trump won the 2016 election. It's because he's better than Hillary Clinton at creating arousal. It would've been really interesting to see him square off against the other arousal king—Bernie Sanders.

This is the same power talk radio hosts tap into to build followers in the tens of millions.

Fire up your readers' emotions and you'll get traffic, shares, and links.

This doesn't always have to mean making people angry. In Chapter 9, we talked about Jonah Berger's book *Contagious*. To refresh, Berger said some emotions like sadness actually discourage action. They do something in our amygdalas that says, "Stay down. Don't do anything. Don't act."

But emotions like fear, anger, joy, love, humor, shock, excitement, and hope encourage action.

Tap into topics with *motivating* emotions and you'll ramp up your chances to get lots of inbound links.

Let's look at *Walmart* as a topic. Plugging that into BuzzSumo, we'll get the most-shared articles with "Walmart" in the title:

(Source: BuzzSumo)

Wow, look at those top most-shared articles! 400,000+ Facebook shares! That's unreal. But every one of them taps a strong emotion—humor, anger, excitement, fear, or shock.

In case you can't quite see the image, here are the top seven:

1. Woman banned from Walmart after riding cart while drinking wine from Pringles can
2. Walmart's "Impeach 45" apparel causes social media outcry, boycott
3. Walmart to host Baby Savings Day on Saturday Feb 23
4. Major Recall Affects Food Sold at Trader Joe's, Walmart and More
5. Arizona Man Accidentally Shoots Himself in Groin at Walmart
6. Walmart sells shotgun shell Christmas lights
7. Walmart's Jet.com is going after Amazon

The two others in the top nine headlines were repeats. I wasn't sure what emotion #7 tapped at first. Now I think it's excitement. (Picture Chris from *Family Guy* reading it, then saying, "Whaaaaaaaat?" Some may find the idea of a Walmart website that works like Amazon exciting. (Imagine shopping without seeing anyone in unflattering Spandex!)

The point?

People share things on social media for the same reason they link to them in articles. Emotion creates motion.

Take that "Impeach 45" title above. That article (from *USA Today*) has 1,247 backlinks from sites like *Vox, Forbes, Snopes, NewsWeek, and MSN.* 1,247 backlinks for *one article!*

Tap into your reader's emotions, and it's a safe bet other content creators will notice and link.

Or—did you know women pay more for products like deodorant and razors?

Why? Is it a lot harder to stop a woman from smelling like a boar than a man? Do women have kevlar leg hair that's extra hard to keep in check?

Cleverly, a little site called ListenMoneyMatters.com wrote a good article about that topic. The site really isn't much. It's got a DA of 58. Not exactly the bestest site in all the land.

But—

It's an inflammatory topic. And they tapped straight into the anger a lot of women feel about the tax. They used language like, "It's a load of crap," and, "Viagra shouldn't be covered by insurance, bitch."

I'm not advocating crudeness, but in this case the writer certainly struck a nerve. (And remember how I said it helps to use the same turns of phrase you find on Reddit if you want to show your empathy?)

As a result, that one article on that one little, low-powered site got 1,579 backlinks from *Vox, Fox, Breitbart, Bustle,* and you get the idea.

Backlink profile for https://www.listenmoneymatters.com/the-pink-tax/
Exact URL

URL rating	Domain rating	Backlinks	Referring domains
40	58	1,580	219
		97% dofollow	86% dofollow

(Source: Ahrefs.com)

Remember, this is not *USA Today*. This is *ListenMoneyMatters*.

Strike a nerve, and you'll strike link paydirt.

4. Shed New Light on Existing Information

How's your insight?

Do you blindly accept what you read? Do you believe what everyone tells you?

I bet you don't.

Chances are you're more like David Crosby. You "question all the answers." You don't slavishly accept the facts you're handed.

Here's another question:

Have you ever had the experience of looking at a simple, palatable explanation and realizing things were a bit more complex? Have you ever realized the "conventional wisdom" wasn't right?

I bet you have.

If you can take existing data and create a new analysis, you've created something new.

What the heck am I talking about?

Remember the movie, *Inception?* It was about Leonardo Di-

Caprio and Ellen Paige and Joseph Gordon-Levitt going into people's dreams within dreams within dreams. The plot was confusing but nobody was quite sure if it was a bad plot or a really good plot so smart they couldn't understand it.

There's a really cool website called Inception Explained that's got a great interactive infographic that explains the plot.

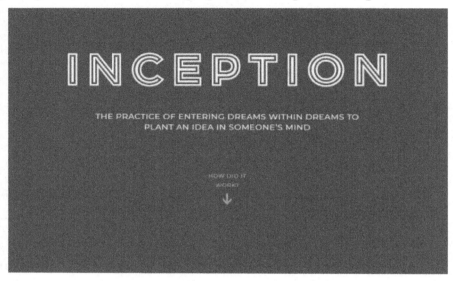

The site is fun to play around with, but it offers an explanation nobody else on the web was giving at the time.

It also does it in a visual way, which is a nice touch. The combination of great visuals and a clear explanation is probably why the site got 1,698 backlinks.

Backlink profile for http://inception-explained.com/
Domain with all its subdomains

Domain rating	Backlinks	Referring domains
52	1,698	398
	72% dofollow	76% dofollow

(Source: Ahrefs.com)

You can do the same thing with sports, stocks, or anything that can be confusing. If you can provide a different analysis of existing information, you can build links.

5. Get Links for the Sake of Getting Links

Would you like Google to respect all the pages on your site more?

You can do that by building pages for the sole purpose of getting links.

What I'm talking about is pure linkbait. Those are pages that get little traffic, but lots of links.

The idea is that if you write a post readers don't care about, but content creators *do* care about it, you'll get links.

Google will see those links and say, "Hey, that page gets a lot of links. We should respect it."

Then by inference, Google will also respect the other pages on your site. You can help the process by linking to your non-respected pages from the respected one. Then Google says, "Hey, that page I respect linked to this other page. I should respect it too."

I don't know how I feel about this practice. It certainly doesn't empathize with the reader. It seems a lot like tricking Google. It seems like a black-hat tactic.

Here are a few types of pure linkbait content:

Guest Posts: These are posts you write for sites with high DA, then put sneaky links in them back to your own site.

Big lists of facts. A big list of sales statistics might not interest many readers, but it'll interest a lot of writers. Write one, and you'll get lots of links.

Big lists of blogs. Write a list of the 50 best business blogs or baby blogs. The bloggers will see the inbound link and link back to you.

"What Is" posts. Define an industry concept or term. Content creators who need to define the term will link to you.

As I said, I'm not crazy about writing "linkbait" posts. They work—currently. But since they don't center around reader empathy or serving the reader best, I don't think they'll work forever. At some point, Google has to start devaluing inbound links to low-traffic content.

The one possible exception is "what is" posts, because some of them do get a lot of traffic.

For example, a company called Stackify writes some great "What is" posts in the programming industry. They write posts called "What is polymorphism" or "What is inheritance?"

I actually wrote one of these posts for them. It was "What Are OOP Concepts in Java?" (It was really hard to write because I'm not a Java programmer." But it ranks #1 in Google and gets 114 backlinks.

Backlink profile for https://stackify.com/oops-concepts-in-java/
Exact URL

URL rating	Domain rating	Backlinks	Referring domains
25	73	114	38
		68% dofollow	55% dofollow

(Source: Ahrefs.com)

Since that article, Stackify's Thorben Janssen has written dozens of "what is" posts. They're excellent articles. They all rank high, and they get tons of inbound links.

But Janssen's articles also get a lot of traffic. According to SEMRush, their "What is Polymorphism" post gets over 40,000 views a month.

So, if that post also gets a ton of links, is there anything "black hat" about that? There doesn't seem to be. The posts are definitely designed to get links, but who cares if they're also helping readers? "What is" posts seem like kind of a win-win.

Backlink profile for https://stackify.com/oop-concept-polymorphism/
Exact URL

URL rating	Domain rating	Backlinks	Referring domains
19	73	61	18
		18% dofollow	44% dofollow

(Source: Ahrefs.com)

Want to know more about building linkbait content? Here are two great articles:

Moz: How to Create Content That Keeps Earning Links (Even After You Stop Promoting It)

Ahrefs: Deconstructing Linkbait: How to Create Content That Attracts Backlinks

Monitor Your Backlinks

All links are good, right?

Nope.

Some links are evil, black-hat links.

Others are low-quality and Google doesn't like them.

You can check the backlinks of any page with the Ahrefs free backlink checker tool. It shows how many links a page has and where they come from.

There's another tool called MajesticSEO that shows a site's

link profile—whether the site's links are good or bad.

If they're bad, you can work to have them removed. You can contact the shady site's administrator and ask them to pull the links. If that doesn't work, you can use Google's Disavow tool to tell Google to ignore the links.

That's all a bit technical and beyond the scope of this book. If you're interested in digging into how to disavow bad backlinks, check out this excellent article from Yoast.

Make Your Own Links

Does linking to your own pages count for SEO?

Sure.

Links from one page of your site to another aren't backlinks, but they definitely count as links.

If you've got a new page that you'd like to rank high, you can link to it from another page on your site that already ranks high.

You'll pass "link juice" from the page with high Page Authority (PA) to the new page.

But—

There's right way and a wrong way.

The wrong way is to link internally for the sake of passing link juice.

The right way is to keep the reader's needs at heart.

Let's say you wrote an article about how to make a budget. From that article, you can link to other articles you wrote about how to track expenses or ways to save on groceries.

But it makes no sense to link to net worth articles or content about real estate investing.

In other words, keep your well-earned reader empathy in mind. If an internal link doesn't help the reader, leave it out.

So—that's all there is to getting backlinks. Yes, there are black-hat ways to get links, but heaven help you if Google catches you. Even if they don't, sooner or later the only links that'll matter are the ones you earn—the ones that show you serve the searcher. In a nutshell, *serve the searcher.* Build something unique and valuable, and you'll draw links aplenty.

There's another way to prove our chops to Google. It's by helping searchers even before they click through to our pages.

CHAPTER 15: SHOW THE SEARCHER YOU CARE BEFORE SHE FINDS YOUR ARTICLE

Ranking #1 is not enough.

Why?

Google created a little wonder called the "featured snippet."

It's an info box that shows up at the top of some search results.

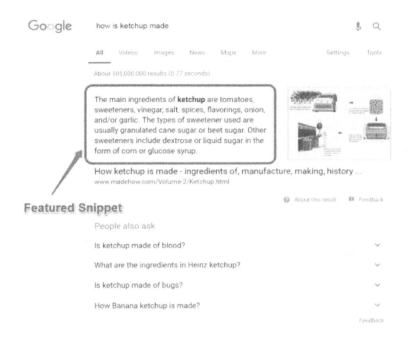

Featured Snippet

(Source: Google.com)

Featured snippets gobble 8.6% of the traffic from each search.

That means if you can rank high *and* get a featured snippet, you can boost your traffic.

The good news? You can convince Google to give you a featured snippet.

Once again, it all comes down to empathy. Understand the searcher, solve the searcher's problem *in the snippet*, and you'll nab the snippet.

Here's how:

1. See if There's Already a Featured Snippet for Your Keyword

First, Google-search your focus keyword. (Nearly all searches have them.) Here's the featured snippet for the term, "real estate invest" from Wikipedia:

"Real estate investing involves the purchase, ownership, management, rental and/or sale of real estate for profit. Improvement of realty property as part of a real estate investment strategy is generally considered to be a sub-specialty of real estate investing called real estate development."

That's not terrible. It answers the searcher's question. But—

Can you do a better job than that?

I'll bet you can. It's not that well-written. It doesn't grab the searcher. It's academic, densely-worded copy.

If you can write a better featured snippet, there's a good chance Google will use yours instead. Then you'll grab that traffic instead of giving it to Wikipedia.

But there's a special way to do it.

2. Make Your Featured Snippet Better Than the Current One

This part isn't rocket science. Just take a good, hard look at the existing featured snippet and see what's wrong with it. Is it missing information? Is it poorly written? Too wordy?

Does the current snippet have lots of big words? Long sentences? Does it make the reader think? Does it miss the point of what the searcher wants to know?

Fix any of these things, and you've got a better featured snippet.

3. Make Your Featured Snippet 40–80 Words Long

A study by SEMRush showed featured snippets are usually between 43 and 86 words in length.

That's just more reader empathy, because an answer that long takes about 10 seconds to read. A good rule of thumb is to keep your snippets short, vibrant, readable, and value-packed.

4. Know Where to Put Your Snippets

Where should you put your featured snippet text? That depends on the kind of snippet you're targeting.

There are several varieties of featured snippet:

- Paragraph snippets: Paragraphs of text that explain or describe the term the searcher typed into Google Search. These can be definitions, explanations, or answers to questions.
- List snippets: Lists that serve "how to" type searches.
- Table snippets: Data displayed in tables.
- Video snippets: Videos usually from YouTube.

If you're going for a featured snippet for your focus keyword, put your snippet text near the top of your article, below the introduction.

If you're trying for a featured snippet around a different keyword that is *not* your focus keyword, put it wherever it serves your reader best.

For most definition, paragraph, and Q/A snippets:

1. Put the keyword first.
2. Add 44 words that describe the keyword or answer the searcher's question.

Let's say we want to grab the snippet for "When did the dinosaurs die?"

Here's the current snippet from a Wikipedia page called "Dinosaur:"

The Cretaceous–Paleogene extinction event, which occurred approximately 66 million years ago at the end of the Cretaceous period, caused the extinction of all dinosaur groups except for the neor-nithine birds.

If you're writing a post specifically about when the dinosaurs died, you'd write your article's introduction, then add something like this before your first section:

When did the dinosaurs die?

Most dinosaurs died out 66 million years ago in an event called the Cretaceous-Paleogene extinction. But some winged dinosaurs called the neornithine birds survived. They became the ancestors of modern birds. They may have avoided destruction thanks to comparatively larger brains.

I'm biased, but I think that's a better snippet. It's closer to 45 words, a little more emotional, and easier to read. It's also got some tantalizing info that the current snippet lacks.

It solves the searcher's problem fast, but then it adds a hook that stands a good chance of getting searchers to click and read my article.

Plus, Google will know it's a snippet because the keyword is right at the top in bold.

As one more benefit, my page is specifically about the timing of dinosaur extinction. Google (and the readers) will likely see that and decide it's a better snippet source than a catchall page from Wikipedia called "Dinosaur."

If I was writing a page called "about the dinosaurs," I'd write the same snippet text. But—I'd put it lower in my article instead of in the introduction.

The same trick works for regular non-question keywords and for definitions. Just add the keywords to your article in bold (or H2, H3, or H4 text) then a roughly 45-word answer below.

5. Make List Snippets Two Ways

Some keyword searches work better with list snippets.

One classic example is the "how to" search.

If you're searching "how to build a birdhouse" or "how to clean a carburetor," a paragraph isn't your best choice. (Actually it's probably a video, but that's for a different book.)

Let's say you're writing a piece on how to end a cover letter. Instead of writing a keyword and paragraph to nab the snippet, write a short, bulleted conclusion at the end of your content.

Here's a featured snippet I wrote that way on Zety.com:

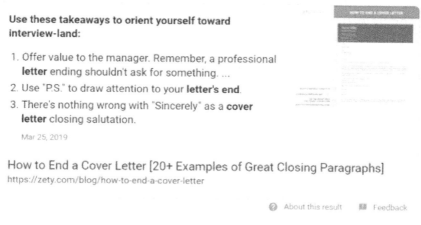

Use these takeaways to orient yourself toward interview-land:

1. Offer value to the manager. Remember, a professional **letter** ending shouldn't ask for something. ...
2. Use "P.S." to draw attention to your **letter's end**.
3. There's nothing wrong with "Sincerely" as a **cover letter** closing salutation.

Mar 25, 2019

How to End a Cover Letter [20+ Examples of Great Closing Paragraphs]
https://zety.com/blog/how-to-end-a-cover-letter

About this result   Feedback

(Source: Google.com)

In case you can't see the image, it says:

Use these takeaways to orient yourself toward interview-land:

1. *Offer value to the manager. Remember, a professional letter ending shouldn't ask for something...*
2. *Use "P.S." to draw attention to your letter's end.*
3. *There's nothing wrong with "Sincerely" as a cover letter closing salutation.*

That's engagingly-written. It's got a couple "aha" moments. It leaves a little room for curiosity, pumping up the chance the searcher will click it.

List snippets like that also work with "best smartphones" or, "best business bloggers" types of articles. But writing a list at the end of your content isn't the only way to get them.

Write "Snippetable" Outlines

Here's a tip:

Google pulls a clever trick sometimes with snippets.

If your content's outline is informative enough, Google will pull the entire outline out and use it as a featured snippet.

For instance, The Muse wrote an article about common interview questions. Their article had no images. It just had numbered headings (H2s) with paragraphs between them.

1. Can you tell me a little about yourself?

This question seems simple, so many people fail to prepare for it, but it's crucial. Here's the deal: Don't give your complete employment (or personal) history. Instead give a pitch—one that's concise and compelling and that shows exactly why you're the right fit for the job. Start off with the 2-3 specific accomplishments or experiences that you most want the interviewer to know about, then wrap up talking about how that prior experience has positioned you for this specific role.

Read More

2. How did you hear about the position?

Another seemingly innocuous interview question, this is actually a perfect opportunity to stand out and show your passion for and connection to the company. For example, if you found out about the gig through a friend or professional contact, name drop that person, then share why you were so excited about it. If you discovered the company through an event or article, share that. Even if you found the listing through a random job board, share what, specifically, caught your eye about the role.

Read More

3. What do you know about the company?

Any candidate can read and regurgitate the company's "About" page. So, when interviewers ask this, they aren't necessarily trying to gauge whether you understand the mission—they want to know whether you care about it. Start with one line that shows you understand the company's goals, using a couple key words and phrases from the website, but then go on to make it personal. Say, "I'm personally drawn to this mission because..." or "I really believe in this approach because..." and share a personal example or two.

Read More

4. Why do you want this job?

Again, companies want to hire people who are passionate about the job, so you should have a great answer about why you want the position. (And if you don't? You probably should apply elsewhere.) First, identify a couple of key factors that make the role a great fit for you (e.g., "I love customer support because I love the constant human interaction and the satisfaction that comes from helping someone solve a problem"), then share why you love the company (e.g., "I've always been passionate about education, and I think you guys are doing great things, so I want to be a part of it").

Read More

Google gave them the featured snippet for the term "common interview questions." To build the snippet, it took their numbered H2s and made them into a list.

How to Answer the 31 Most Common Interview Questions

1. Can you tell me a little about yourself? ...
2. How did you hear about the position? ...
3. What do you know about the company? ...
4. Why do you want this **job**? ...
5. Why should we hire you? ...
6. What are your greatest professional strengths? ...
7. What do you consider to be your weaknesses?

   More items...

31 Common Interview Questions and Answers - The Muse
https://www.themuse.com/.../how-to-answer-the-31-most-common-interview-questions

behavioral   for managers   engineering   customer service   finance   for market

About this result   Feedback

(Source: Google.com)

Google actually used their outline as a snippet.

It's got a list of the seven most common interview questions. That fits the searcher's needs nicely, but it also leaves us wanting more (so we click the link).

The point? Pay attention to your section headings (H2s). If your focus keyword is best served with a list-type answer, number your H2s and craft them as if you were writing a list best suited to the search itself. Do it well enough, and there's a good chance Google will reward you.

Want to dig deeper into how to nab featured snippets with your articles? A.J. Ghergich at SEMRush wrote an awesome ultimate guide.

The main point about featured snippets when it comes to

SEO? They're ways to show the searcher we've got what she needs before she even finds our page. Even if we rank at the bottom of page 1 of the Google results, we can still grab a featured snippet if we write them better than the current offerings.

Do it right, and you'll snap up 8% of the search traffic for the term, plus whatever else you get for your position on page 1.

The takeaway? Getting Google's featured snippets is a great way to harness extra traffic. With a little effort into how we structure our content, we can write ready-made snippets that boost the chances Google will put us in the pet-shop window.

Next let's look at how to answer lots of reader questions with one article, and get a lot more traffic.

CHAPTER 16: SERVE THE SEARCHER MORE BY RANKING FOR LOTS OF KEYWORDS (NOT JUST ONE)

You want lots of traffic, right?

Well—

Remember *Superman III?*

No? Okay, I'm ancient. I get AARP membership applications like most people get credit card offers.

Well, then, remember *Office Space?*

Office Space quotes *Superman III.* Specifically, it quotes the part where Richard Pryor writes a harmless little piece of computer code that rounds up all the fractions-of-a-cent from electronic bank transactions and deposits them in his account.

I don't remember what happens to Pryor's character. I think he builds an improbable and poorly-rendered computer menace that Superman has a hard time fighting for some reason (though I often find it challenging to get mine to switch between browser tabs).

But in Office Space, Ron Livingston's character winds up with $305,326.13.

What in the blue monkey does this have to do with SEO?

Well, we're about to pull that kind of trick with website traffic.

If that sounds nefarious, it's not. We're not going to black-hat 1/1000th of every website visitor and shunt them to our pages.

What we'll do is help lots of readers who aren't getting served, by adding little, random keywords only a few people a month are looking for.

They're called "long tail keywords," and there's a trick to getting traffic from them.

Don't Bet the Farm

You wouldn't want to write a whole article around a keyword that only gets 10 searches a month. Remember Chapter 5: Pick Topics That Start a Traffic-lanche? In that chapter we learned to pick a focus keyword that our article is "about."

Let's say your focus keyword is "breakfast cereals." About 8,100 people every month search for that term. If you rank #1, that's great.

But there are hundreds of related keywords with monthly traffic from 6,600 all the way down to 3. Here are a few:

- Bran cereal
- Wheat cereal
- Granola cereal
- Hot cereal
- Fiber cereal
- Low calorie cereal
- Cereal grains
- Is cereal healthy
- And so on

They've all got a lot less traffic than "breakfast cereals," but there are literally thousands of related terms. Total up all the traffic for all of them and you've got almost 70,000 searches every month.

That's a lot more traffic than just "breakfast cereals" at 6,600. More than ten times more traffic.

Can you rank for all those terms? No. You'd drive yourself batty trying.

Can you rank for lots of them?

You bet.

Find Stacks of Long-Tail Keywords

Long-tail keywords are the last kid picked. They're the sad, lonely keywords almost nobody is looking for. They're hanging out by the bleachers at the school dance and nobody will dance with them.

But here's the mind-blower:

The overwhelming majority of Google searches are long-tail searches.

So those popular-kid keywords? The ones with the white smiles and the perfect hair that get a ton of traffic?

Put together, the long-tail keywords dwarf them.

Keyword research site Ahrefs analyzed 1.9 billion keywords in their database. They found out over 92% get less than ten searches every month.

That means only 8% of keywords are *not* long-tail keywords.

And guess what?

Nobody is trying very hard to rank for those long-tails.

Serve the people who are interested in unpopular keywords, and you can get a ton of traffic.

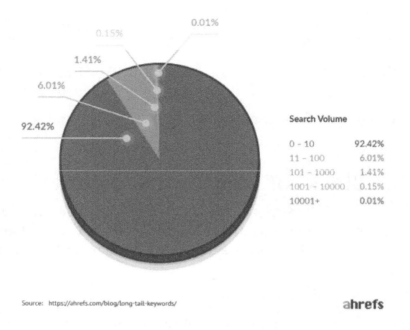

Monthly Search Volume Distribution of 1.9 Billion Search Queries

Search Volume	
0 - 10	92.42%
11 - 100	6.01%
101 - 1000	1.41%
1001 - 10000	0.15%
10001+	0.01%

Source: https://ahrefs.com/blog/long-tail-keywords/

ahrefs

Those "unpopular" keywords own 92% of all the traffic on the internet.

So how do we get them?

Follow the steps below.

1. Look in Your Keyword Research

When you do your keyword research in Ahrefs (or SEMRush or Grepwords), you'll type your focus keyword in the search box. Ahrefs will give you a list of keywords, ranked by monthly traffic. (Remember that you can export that list as a spreadsheet.)

Look at all the related keywords that trail off in a long tail from your focus keyword. They're all great long-tail keywords to try for.

2. Look in Google's Autocomplete Results

When you type a search in Google's box, Google tries to guess what you're trying to say. We've all seen funny examples of it. There's even a page of 77 absurd Google Autocompletes at runt-of-the-web.com. One of my favorites is that someone typed in, "Why isn't" and Google suggested, "Why isn't 11 pronounced onety one."

But Google's autocomplete results are good for more than just a laugh. They're great for finding long-tail keywords too.

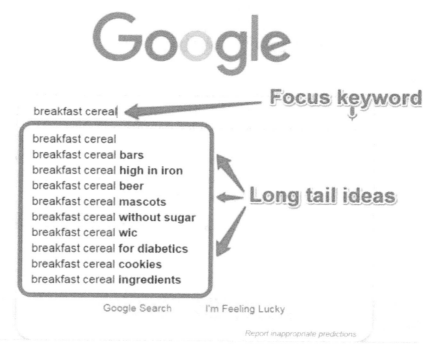

(Source: Google.com)

I typed in "breakfast cereals" and got:

- Bars

High in iron
- Breakfast cereal beer (ay?)
- Breakfast cereal mascots
- Breakfast cereal without sugar
- Breakfast cereal wic

And so on.

3. Use Google's People Also Ask

Back in Chapter 4, we used Google's "People Also Ask" to scrape a list of questions related to our focus keyword.

Those are almost always long-tail keywords. Why? Because they aren't getting answered. They have such low traffic nobody online has bothered to address them yet.

4. Use Answer the Public or Ahrefs

Ahrefs (and the other KR tools) all have "Question" tabs that show a list of questions related to your focus keyword. Scoop those up and drop them in a column of your KR spreadsheet. They often make good long tail keywords.

A creepy but useful site called Answer the Public does the same thing. You can search any term you want, then download a CSV file stuffed with related terms.

5. Check Your Long-Tail Keywords

Not every keyword from our research will be a long-tail keyword. Some already have dedicated articles.

How can you tell?

Unfortunately you have to Google them.

You won't have time to Google-search every keyword in your list. Doing that would take more time than any content creator has. But you should know you won't rank for every keyword on your list.

For example, look at "breakfast cereal mascots" from our search above.

Google's first page of results has 10 articles specifically about breakfast cereal mascots.

(Source: Google.com)

So—we're not likely to rank for that long-tail keyword. We can cross that one off our list.

Rank for the Long-Tail Keywords in Your List

Finding long-tail keywords is one thing. But how do we turn them into traffic?

Here's the very good news:

Long-tail keywords are a lot easier to rank for than their high-school quarterback cousins. Remember, they're not the track star or the cheerleading team captain. They're flugelhorn #4 in the marching band. Other content creators aren't writing articles about them. Ask them to dance and they're all yours.

But there's a trick to it.

We don't want to spend 2–5 hours writing a 1,000-word or 2,500-word article about a long-tail keyword with 10 searches a month. That's maximum effort for minimal return.

Well, we don't have to.

If you can rank for your focus keyword, you've got a sky-high shot at ranking for all the long-tail keywords that come with it.

But here's the thing:

You've got an even higher shot at ranking for those long-tail keywords if you try to capture them on purpose.

That comes back to using empathy to serve our reader.

Do that by putting long-tail keywords in your headings, subheadings, bullet lists, images, bolded text, and tables.

Start With Outlining

When outlining, use your focus keyword and your long-tail

keywords as your guide. Start with the most important (i.e. highest traffic) keyword.

Headings

To target long-tail keywords in your headings, put the ones with the most traffic in your biggest headings, highest in your article.

I had to write an article for Zety.com about how to address a cover letter.

Among my long-tail keywords list were:

- How to address a cover letter with no name
- Who to address a cover letter to
- Cover letter dear
- Cover letter Mrs.
- Cover letter email address

And so on.

So I did some thinking. My searcher, Alice, might find my article by searching any of the terms above. But—she was interested in *all* of them.

Because of the traffic numbers in my KR, I knew she cared more about some terms and less about others. So I outlined my article to put the more important terms in my section headings (H2s) and sub-headings (H3s, H4s).

My article now ranks #2 for the main term, but it also ranks high for the others. Why?

Because I built the article to serve the searcher. Alice can find the article by searching any of those terms, start skimming, and see right away she's in the right place.

You're already doing this if you read Chapter 11: Empathy Through Better Structure. Now you know it has a powerful secondary effect of getting your content to rank for lots of different keyword searches.

Get Multiple Featured Snippets

To me, the most exciting part about ranking for multiple keywords is grabbing multiple featured snippets.

In Chapter 15 we talked about nabbing featured snippets. We said if we can write a bullet list or a 45-word paragraph that serves a keyword, we can often grab the featured snippet for it.

But if we use subheadings and bullet lists right, we can rank for multiple featured snippets with one article.

It's easy.

Take a long-tail keyword that you know your reader is interested in. Then put it in a subheading like an H3 or an H4. Then write a 45-word explanation of the term right under it, or a 5–7 line bullet list like we discussed in the last chapter.

There's a good chance Google will grab your list or paragraph and use it as a featured snippet—even if it's not your focus keyword.

(Source: Google.com)

Images

If you can see the image above, you'll see the snippet isn't just text. Google put an image near the text is an image. It found the image in my article. The image title is how_to_address_a_cover_letter.

The image is a very useful infographic that breaks down how to address a cover letter. It's packed with useful information.

Google doesn't always grab its snippet text and image from the same page, though. If an image from someone else's page served the reader better, Google would have grabbed that one instead.

For instance, I just searched "how to use smart plugs." I got a text snippet from constellation.com. It's a bullet list.

But Google also served up an image of a smart plug, phone, and what looks like a coffee pot. That image is from an article on makeuseof.com called "10 Creative Uses for Smart Plugs That'll Make You Want One."

(Source: Google.com)

The image is useful because it gives new information. It shows a smart plug, coffee pot, and smartphone. On the smartphone are controls for porch lights, coffee, a fan, and a motion sensor. These are all good ideas for using smart plugs. I believe the usefulness of the image is why it found its way into Featured Snippet stardom. Readers like it and click it often because it helps answer their question, just by glancing at it.

To boost your chance of getting your images into featured snippets:

1. Make them useful. Use your KR and long-tail keyword list to build images jam-packed with information.
2. Name your images with long-tail keywords. That's another signal to Google to spray you with the featured-snippet hose.

So make your images useful and eye-catching based on your understanding of the searcher's needs, and you're likely to get a lot more featured snippets for a lot more keywords.

Bolded Text and Tables

Here are two more ways to turn searchers and skimmers into readers:

Build long-tail keywords into 1) bolded text and 2) tables.

When skimmers zip through your article, they'll skip most of the text, focusing on H2s, H3s, lists, tables, images, and bolded content.

Putting long-tail keywords in your bolded text and tables is another way to catch that reader's eye. If she comes looking for a long-tail keyword, she'll be more likely to find it if it's in bold or in a table.

As you build your outline from keywords, keep coming back to search intent. Does your reader care about these things? Use your keyword research to understand the reader first. Then build your outline and structure around those keywords. But when you're done, take a minute to step back and look at it from the reader's point of view.

Does your structure serve the reader in the best possible way? Does it empathize with what she's trying to find out?

If not, adjust. If it comes down to a choice between sticking to your long-tail-keyword-generated outline and serving the reader, always go with serving the reader first.

PART 5: CONVERTING AND "STANDARD" SEO

CHAPTER 17: WRITE CONTENT THAT CONVERTS

Ready for a shock?

Traffic doesn't mean money.

Yes, our primary focus with creating content is empathy. We want to understand the searcher and write articles that serve her needs.

I'll admit there may be the odd millionaire out there doing it solely for the good of humankind. But the rest of us need to eat. Even altruistic cancer researchers need a paycheck if they want to keep drawing breath so they can do more cancer research.

So it's not enough just to get a pile of traffic.

That traffic has to turn into money at some point or it's good for nothing.

I've got two examples direct from my real life about how this can blow up in your face.

It Happened to Me

My first sad story was with the money site. Over a period of 18 months, I wrote hundreds of articles that amassed a total traffic count of 600,000 per month. Astounding! Every month, my words were reaching enough searchers to fill six football stadiums.

But we weren't breaking even.

At least I think we weren't. The owner never shared revenue data with me, but I did some calculations based on traffic and ad revenue estimates. The result I got did not excite me.

The problem? We weren't selling anything. The site was monetized from ad revenue. After they paid a salary to me and my editor, there was probably nothing left. In fact we were most likely operating at a small deficit.

That's kind of crazy, isn't it? But it's exactly why sites like *BuzzFeed* had to lay off all those people in early 2019.

Frankly, ad revenue isn't the best way to monetize a blog. Ad revenue isn't huge, and it's shrinking all the time.

By far a better way to make money from a website is if you have a product to sell (i.e. content marketing).

Why does this matter to you as a content creator?

Because it helps us shape our content. It shows us we need to write content that turns searchers into skimmers into readers and then finally into buyers.

It Happened to Me Again

After the money site folded I went to work for a medical waste blog for a couple months. They had monthly traffic of about 8,000 a month and I raised it to about 45,000 in a very short time. They were ecstatic.

I was happy too, because their revenue wasn't ad-based. They were selling an actual product. That meant they didn't need 600,000 monthly visits to make money. Even if they only got 500 visits a month, they'd be sitting pretty if all those 500 people signed up for their medical waste disposal service.

So, they asked me to target medical people like doctors, clinic owners, and medical administrators.

I did some phone work. I called dozens of their customers and built a spreadsheet with their job titles. I interviewed them about their internet-usage habits. I tried to build a picture of what kinds of articles would interest them.

Then I did a lot of keyword research to identify the best topics for them that would generate the most traffic.

Finally, I used KR, CA, and SMA to write a lot of high-ranking, high-traffic articles. I ranked #1 for "what is medical waste," "hip replacement videos," "bad medical reviews," "HIPAA violation cases," and dozens of other terms.

I was thrilled. *They* were thrilled. I'd got tons of new traffic for them, targeted to the kinds of people who needed their service.

But here's where it all fell down:

None of my articles converted.

See, there was a CTA on each of my pages that said something like, "Hey, do you need medical waste disposal service? We do a great job at reasonable rates. Click here!"

But nobody was clicking.

Why not? Why weren't we converting?

At the time we didn't know. We only knew that all my beautiful, targeted traffic wasn't turning into money.

They decided to discontinue the experiment. I stopped working for them while they tried to figure out a better use for their marketing dollars. Meanwhile I went to work for Zety.com.

To Convert, Know Your Purchasing Funnel and Use It

Here's the problem:

When I got all that great traffic for the medical site, it wasn't the right *kind* of traffic.

Yes, it was the right people. It was doctors, clinic owners, head nurses, administrators, and other high-ranking health practitioners. It was the kind of people who need medical waste disposal services.

But it wasn't hitting them at the right time.

With the benefit of years of hindsight, I believe that even though my pages weren't converting, they were (and still are) doing the site a lot of good.

Those pages are drawing high-quality backlinks. They're raising the site's Domain Authority (DA). They're also raising awareness for the company's brand with people who *might* become their clients later when the time is right.

I think the company knows this too. They've made me two offers to come back since then and work on various projects, though I've been too busy with Zety to accept.

The real reason my pages didn't convert is that they were catching people at the top of the purchasing funnel.

What's a purchasing funnel?

It's a marketing concept that describes how we make buying decisions.

There are different ways to use it, depending on what part of sales and marketing you're talking about. For our purposes, we'll use it to talk about searchers vs buyers.

The funnel has a top, a middle, and a bottom.

At the top of the funnel are people who aren't ready to buy anything. At the bottom are people who are actively looking to buy what you're selling. It goes like this:

- Awareness
- Interest
- Desire

- Action

My articles were great. They were targeting the right people. But they were targeting them when they were at the top of the funnel. They were reaching readers at the "awareness" stage.

My readers were aware that they had medical waste, but they weren't ready to buy our service. They probably already had a service they were satisfied with.

The Purchase Funnel

(Source: Wikimedia.org)

So, they liked my articles a lot, but they weren't looking to buy.

This matters to us as content creators because it helps us pick our content.

It's not enough just to pick high-traffic topics and write great, empathy-packed articles that rank high for those terms.

We also have to be very directed about whether we're writing articles to build our domain authority or to generate conversion into sales.

There's nothing wrong with writing articles that rank #1 for terms like, "what is medical waste" with no hope of converting.

If the article gets backlinks, raises our DA, and makes lots of potential future customers more aware of our brand, great.

But there's something wrong with writing only articles that don't convert. At some point the money has to flow in or the whole project goes belly-up.

So how do we write articles that hit our readers at the bottom of the purchasing funnel?

We give a lot of thought to the kinds of topics our customers are likely to be searching just before they buy.

The medical waste blog I worked for had great success targeting local search terms like, "medical waste disposal Boise Idaho" and "medical waste disposal Waterville Maine." They wrote hundreds of articles like that and dominated the search terms. I've seen a national resume-writing firm use the same technique with great success.

Zety is a Software-as-a-Service (SaaS) that sells an online resume-and-cover-letter builder. To intercept customers at the bottom of the purchasing funnel, we write a lot of articles about how to write resumes for different jobs.

If I went back to work for the medical waste site now, I'd find the frustrations of the company's potential customers who are very low in the funnel. I'd write articles with much lower monthly traffic but much higher conversion potential.

I know lots of medical waste companies have unfair contracts squeeze their customers, so I'd write articles about medical waste law. I know healthcare providers are worried who's at fault when they pass their waste to a disposal service that then breaks the law, so I'd write articles about that. I'd find the fear points, anger points, and other emotional triggers of searchers who aren't satisfied with their current medical waste disposal solution, and I'd write stacks of articles to serve them.

Pick your topics this way, then write them with a ton of reader empathy, and you'll convert like a house afire.

Of course you also need great CTAs (Calls to Action) on your pages. That's outside the scope of this book, but if you're interested there's a good article about it at CrazyEgg.

To write traffic that converts, the key point is to know your customers. Know their needs. Know what kinds of questions they ask right before they buy. Then write articles that solve those problems.

Here's a tip:

You can do that for more than just one search term with a single article.

CHAPTER 18:
METADATA, ETC.

Well, this part had to go somewhere.

As I was writing this book, I got an email from a fellow journalist. She said a corporate client asked her if she knew how to write metadata. She didn't know what metadata was.

Metadata is all the stuff that's not part of your content that helps Google understand what your article is about.

It's kind of like a job application, except it's your application to get ranked in Google.

Do it right, and it can help you rank.

Do it wrong, and Google might punt your pages even if they're beautifully conceived and executed.

We'll go through the basics in this (very short) chapter, just in case you're interested.

If you're a content creator who's been asked to add metadata, chances are you won't be adding it in straight HTML.

You'll probably need to add it in WordPress and/or the Yoast SEO plugin. It's pretty simple. We'll go through it all here.

SEO Title

A blog post's "SEO Title" is just the title of the article. The HTML code of the page puts the title in a special HTML element called a "Title Tag." With WordPress, you don't have to worry about HTML. Just enter your title tag directly into the title box. WordPress will snag it from there and use it as the title tag in your metadata.

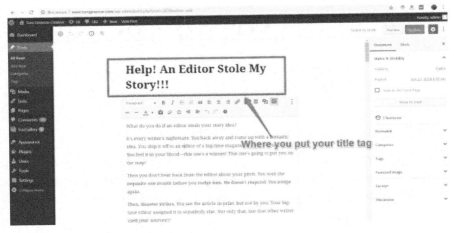

(Source: WordPress.com)

Slug

In SEO parlance, a slug isn't something that eats your basil plants at night. It's part of the link that leads to your page.

For instance, the URL of my website is www.tomgerencer.com. I have a page on the site that lists all my clients and publications. The URL for that page is http://www.tomgerencer.com/clients-publications/

The "slug" is the little part at the end of the normal URL that leads to my page: /clients-publications/.

So in a nutshell:

- Site URL: www.tomgerencer.com
- Page URL: http://www.tomgerencer.com/clients-publications/
- Page Slug: /clients-publications/

Why would you care in a million years?

Some people think it matters for SEO. I think it used to matter a lot, and it may matter some still. Site owners and editors often write the slugs themselves, but in case that duty falls in your lap, here's why slugs matter:

Slugs are a way of telling Google what you hope to rank for. Writing a slug that contains your focus keyword won't guarantee you'll rank.

What it *will* do is say, "Hey, Google, I'm trying to rank for this term."

That may or may not help SEO. I believe it at least stops Google from getting confused about your intentions.

The Yoast SEO plugin outlines some SEO best practices for writing slugs:

- **Don't use stop words.** Words like "a" and "and" are extra. They're not keywords, so we shouldn't include them in our slugs.
- **Keep it keywordy.** If your topic is "best breakfast cereals," then your slug should be something like, "best-breakfast-cereals," not, "best-breakfast-cereals-money-can-buy."
- **Make it Descriptive.** Someone should be able to glance at your slug and know exactly what your article is about.

You can also edit your page's slug in WordPress without using Yoast. WordPress calls it a "permalink," and it's in the right-side menu bar on every page's editor screen.

(Source: WordPress.com)

Meta Description

A meta description is a short paragraph stored in an HTML page that summarizes the content on the page.

The theory is that Google will take that meta description and put it in the search results. So when you see a page of Google search results, all the little paragraphs under the article titles are the meta descriptions.

In theory.

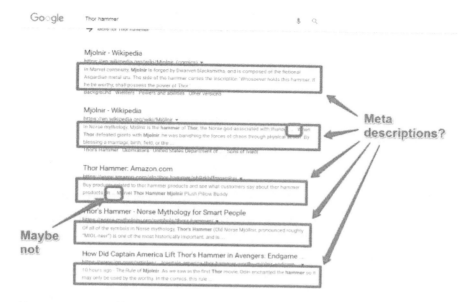

(Source: Google.com)

In reality, Google uses meta descriptions in its search results about 20% of the time. That's based on my own observations, so I'll admit I may be biased.

But if we Google "Thor's hammer," It's clear that at least some of the results that pop up don't take their article descriptions from the pages' meta descriptions.

How do I know that?

Because some of the paragraphs have little ellipses in them—the little cluster of three dots that shows a break between two sentences.

Those ellipses are our clue that Google built its article description by merging two sentences from the text of the article.

In fact most of the other article descriptions on Google's first page of results here also came straight from the pages they're describing.

In other words, you can write meta descriptions if you like. Google may use them, but it most often won't.

But since it's not that hard to do, and since it *might* help, it's not a bad idea to do it anyway.

According to Yoast (and personal experience) meta descriptions should be:

- 155–165 characters in length
- Engagingly-written
- Contain the focus keyword and possibly other keywords
- Show empathy for the reader's problem and pain

They should also outdo the other descriptions on the pages that already rank on page one of Google for your topic. They should show the better mousetrap you've created. The target you're aiming for is to make the reader say, "Oh, wow. That's exactly what I'm looking for."

The Yoast plugin in WordPress has a box where you can type your meta description. It's even labeled, "Meta description" to make life easy.

Image Titles

Writing good image titles can help your SEO.

If you're sticking to the rule of adding only images that bring value to your reader, writing good image titles is easy.

For instance, in an article about lowering employee turnover, a graph that shows employee turnover by country is very useful.

By contrast, a still shot of a disgruntled-looking employee at a desk, breaking a pencil, is not.

You'll most likely name your graph something like, "employee turnover by country." That's natural, right?

Well, Google will see that and think, "Hey, this seems to fit the topic of the article."

And it'll push the article a little higher in its estimation—at least initially.

But the searchers will have final say. If you've got lots of unhelpful images of people breaking pencils in your article, it doesn't matter what you name them. The searchers will find your article a little less useful. They'll tend to click back a bit more. (Unless the pencil-breaking resonates with them emotionally and makes them want to stay. I'm waffling on that.)

But if you've got lots of value-adding images in your article and they're named descriptively, Google will like them and the searchers will concur. Win-win.

As a side-benefit, good titles give your images a chance to rank in Google's image search. Rank high there and you can bring more traffic to your pages. And here's a fun tip: it's often really easy to rank high in Google image search, maybe because so few content creators pay attention to their image titles.

Image Alt Tags

Images have meta data called "alt tags."

Why shouldn't you be yawning, putting down this book, and checking Twitter?

Because alt tags matter to the visually impaired. Screen readers use them to explain a page's images.

SEO pros also think they matter to Google.

The theory is that keywords in a page's alt tags help the page's rankings. It may also help an image rank high in Google's image search.

But—don't stuff your alt tags with keywords. Just use them as intended—to help the visually impaired.

Keep them to 125 characters because screen readers cut off anything longer than that. Use keywords when they fit in naturally with what you're trying to describe, but write a description of the image as if you were explaining it to someone who can't see.

In WordPress, you can enter the alt text for any image by clicking on the image, then clicking the little pencil icon that pops up.

(Source: WordPress.com)

Categories

Each time you create a new post in content, you can assign a category to it.

Site owners can create as many categories as they like.

In a money site, categories might be things like "save money," "net worth," "budgeting," "make money," and, "credit cards."

They may help SEO by keeping like pages grouped. If you're interested in learning more, WordPress Beginner has a good article on them.

(Source: WordPress.com)

Meta Keywords

As a content creator, this will be your nightmare.

Site owners will tell you to add meta keywords to your posts.

Yet every SEO guru and her sister is out there saying, "do not bother."

Google and Bing are also saying, "we don't use them."

Well—do it if it makes the client happy.

If you really want to know how to add them, WordPress Beginner has a page for that, too.

Tags, Featured Images, and Excerpts

There are three more meta data items in the WordPress editor's right-side menu bar. Let's get them over with, shall we? I've provided a link to each in case you want to get into the details and you think I'm glossing over them too much.

- **Tags.** These are words that show a page's topic. They help WordPress group your pages by topic area.
- **Featured Images.** Every page in WordPress should have a featured image. It's the image at the top of the post. Does it help SEO? Maybe peripherally.
- **Excerpts.** These are short paragraphs that describe your post. Google doesn't use them, but your WordPress blog will use them in your main blog page.

Basically, all these things don't matter nearly as much as all the other SEO information in this book, but they do matter. They're not hard to manage, so do them, but don't be afraid of making a mistake.

One more topic you may be interested in is local search marketing. That's outside the scope of this book, but I'd be slacking if I didn't at least point you in the right direction. Moz has a great 5-part guide on local search. It's really important if you're a local business trying to get local customers. The link is right here.

That's all I'll cover about metadata in this book. If you want to dig into it in more detail, check out the excellent book *SEO for Dummies* by Peter Kent.

CONCLUSION

So that's it. SEO is all about building empathy, then proving it to searchers, skimmers, readers, and Google. The better we do it, the higher our pages will rank.

It starts with learning who the searcher is and why she's searching. We do that by doing Keyword Research (KR), Competitive Analysis (CA), and Social Media Analysis (SMA).

A mix of all those methods lets us see the reader's problem and the emotion that put her into motion, driving her to type her search term into Google's input box.

Once we understand her needs, we use the information we collected through our research to solve the reader's problem. We look at the existing offerings, see what's wrong with them or how they miss the point, and build a better mousetrap.

Once we've laid the plans, we structure our great, useful content so the skimmer sees at a glance she's in the right place. We write great headings and sub-headings and add useful images and bullet lists.

The skimmer then becomes a reader. Because we've taken the time to find better information, the reader's needs are filled to the extent she stays with us for five minutes, ten minutes, fifteen minutes or more. Google sees that happen and nudges us a little higher in the search results.

The better we do this, the more other pages link to our uniquely valuable solutions and the better Google likes them.

This is SEO. It's not a lot of keywords laced throughout an

article in a mathematical formula. It's one human heart connected to another—albeit using advanced tools and data to get to the end result.

About the author

Tom Gerencer writes about business, careers, the outdoors, and science. He's a career expert at Zety.com and a regular contributor to Boys' Life and Scouting magazines. His work has been featured in The Costco Connection, Fast Company, Living the Country Life, and Backpacker. His clients include HP, HID, Raytheon, and many more. A Maine native, he lives and works in West Virginia with his wife, two boys, and a couple of ornery dogs.

Acknowledgements

Nobody writes a book alone. I owe a huge debt to my wife Kathy, the biggest-hearted person I know, and to our two boys Maddox and Ben, who always understand when Daddy's working.

This book owes a great debt to Kuba Koziej of Zety.com, who gave me an on-the-run master's degree in SEO, and to Bart Turczynski, also of Zety.com, the best editor I ever had.

This book wouldn't exist without the dozens of SEO professionals who published excellent articles online that taught me so much over the years. I've linked to many of your articles throughout the text. Thank you all.

And of course there are the hundreds of people who've been kind to me and helped me through the years. You know who you are and I appreciate you deeply.

Most of all, thank you to Bill and Jeanne Gerencer, without whom I would not have been me, but possibly someone else, like for instance Sirhan Sirhan or the Earl of Sandwich.

APP to record call : TAPEACALL
TEMI - upload here So cheap AI transcript
that's 90% correct

1. Check who's dominating your topic on Google + check their DA + if similar to yrs you can compete

2. Moz Bar Plugin - ~~Google Chrome~~ to check DA/PA for a specific page URL on the topic

3. Find competition (SEM Rush or Ahrefs) + type in ~~for~~ URL of competition + search their highest-Traffic Keywords (w. at least 1K/mo searches)

4. Look for soft spots (Moz Plugin to see DA of top contenders); if all higher than u maybe walk away. If not u found a soft spot + write article w. ea of top 3-5 terms

5. Look at top article + the reader's ~~problems~~ its addressing + the info/advice/tips given + skim other top 10 articles for more tidbits + then see what they did wrong or didn't cover

6. Armed w. yr. high-traffic topic/keyword research + competitive analysis Spend 20 min. ~~off~~ by ~~Google~~ Searching your topic + the word "Reddit" to see into reader's heart + find trends/common themes/questions/ complaints + tips from pros + how yr. reader talks ie. went nuclear on me' 'the worst' + add those to yr. article.

7. More Insights on Quora - also look at Specialty forums

8. BuzzSumo (a few free searches/day) to see reader feelings. Type in topic + see most shared →

content on social media.

9. BuzzSumo.com - Type in URL of top blogs in yr. industry then see what the most shared articles are

10. Check Google Trends to see if a particular article may below all yr + then trend very high at 1 pt.

11. Streamline ALL (↑) list KR - TOP 10 + key findings from (A/SMA) + mo. traffic estimates (p. 8)

12. TO BE BETTER (p. 90) - 1 tip Make ea. nugget a single point lesson delivering it

13. TIP: Most shared articles create arousal: laughter, anxiety, anger, happiness

FORMULAE (PAS) Problem - describe in detail
(p. 101) Agitate - define the emotions felt by reader b/c of probl
Solution - promise to fix probl

Formulae (BAB) Before-after-Bridge
1. Before: The reader's world now
2. After: what it would feel like to solve probl
3. Bridge: How to do it
Formulae AIDA

Made in the USA
Las Vegas, NV
12 February 2021